ORTHODOX SAINTS

SPIRITUAL PROFILES FOR MODERN MAN

by

GEORGE POULOS

HOLY CROSS ORTHODOX PRESS
Brookline, Massachusetts 02146

Icon Drawings and Initial Cross Designs
courtesy of
DEMETRIOS DUKAS

Cover Design
by
CONSTANTINE N. VAPORIS

Library of Congress Catalog Card No. 76-55954

Published by the Holy Cross Orthodox Press
50 Goddard Avenue
Brookline, Massachusetts 02146

ISBN 0-916586-05-7

TO THE CHERISHED MEMORY OF ARCHBISHOP ATHENAGORAS CAVADAS, BELOVED OF GOD, COMPLETE THEOLOGIAN, BENEVOLENT TEACHER, BUT FOR WHOM THE AUTHOR WOULD NEVER HAVE CLASPED A CHALICE, THIS BOOK IS REVERENTLY DEDICATED

CONTENTS

FOREWORD

History is little more than a study of those who made it; in this sense there can be no complete knowledge of Christianity without at least an acquaintance with the lives of the men and women who shaped the Church through a complete dedication to the service of Jesus Christ. These men and women from the early Disciples down through the ages to the neo-martyrs who have been canonized in recognition of their total dedication to the Messiah are more than a mass of names that appear on religious calendars. They are flesh and blood human beings who acted above and beyond the call of Christian duty; some of their lives have been commonplace and some have been excitingly adventurous, in direct contrast to the concept of a saint kneeling in constant prayer. There are so many saints who don't appear on icons whose spirited lives offer anything but dull reading, and who have comprised the greatest minds and hearts in all mankind. In fact, Christianity itself suffers from a Christian's ignorance of these good folks, which is tantamount to an awareness of Jesus Christ Himself.

To know and to understand the saints of the Church is to know and to understand the Savior better. Who among us does not feel the presence of the Messiah through the reading of SS. Peter and Paul, His greatest Apostles. It is regrettable that the average Christian can call out the names in the lineup of his favorite baseball team, but cannot call to mind the twelve who were on the Savior's varsity, but for whom it might be a different ball game, as the saying goes.

It is not the purpose of this book to chide or admonish, but rather it is hoped that these sketches will be read from time to time and that they will bring us all to a clearer understanding of our existence that we may never lose sight of Jesus Christ.

SAINT BASIL

Δ. DUKAS
1976

St. Basil the Great

The Christian community of the fourth century, struggling for survival against vast odds, found renewed hope and inspiration in the noble efforts of a family of six children, all of whom became saints of the Church. From this remarkable Christian family came St. Basil the Great, a spiritual giant.

Many men in history have had the superlative 'great' added to their names primarily because they were monarchs such as Alexander the Great whose exploits spanned large land masses. St. Basil, however, earned this title for reaching the masses with the word of Christ. He was not a king, but he won the hearts of his fellowmen for service to the King of Kings. The title 'Great' was no more richly deserved by any man in history, for he possessed the humility of Moses, the zeal of Elijah, the faith of Peter, the eloquence of John the Theologian, and the dedication of Paul. St. Basil's brothers and sisters, priests, bishops, and nuns served under his leadership as true workers in the vineyard of Christ.

Born in Caesarea, Asia Minor in A.D. 330, Basil was reared by parents of unusual devotion: they imparted their love of God to their children with such success that each came to be canonized. These six branches of the family tree were bountifully blessed and brought forth much spiritual fruit. St. Basil's spiritual heritage was bequeathed to the Christian community by his life of immeasurable religious expression. He was educated in such cultural centers of the Empire as Constantinople and Athens. Under the guidance of his friend Gregory of Nazianzos, Basil became one of Christianity's most eloquent spokesmen, earning world renown for both his oratory and his writings.

Although he could have had any high governmental position he wished, St. Basil had no desire for high office. Instead he was granted his wish to return to his native city, where he was ordained Bishop of Caesarea on 14 June 370.

A man of considerable talent, Basil applied himself to establishing and setting down the rules of monasticism. With this accomplished, he turned to the formalization of the Divine Liturgy which bears his name. The Liturgy of St. Basil became the standard of Orthodox worship. In fact, the Liturgy of St. John Chrysostom which is celebrated forty-two Sundays of the year, is a condensed version of it. The Liturgy of St. Basil is celebrated on more solemn Church observances, including Christmas and his feast day on January 1, as well as during the Lenten period. St. Basil's Liturgy is thus used a total of ten times during the Church year.

An innovator as well as a creator and planner, Basil was the first to fulfill the desperate need for charitable institutions; he directed the creation and development of orphanages, hospitals, and homes for the aged. His concept of mutual love and respect and his practical application of brotherly love later led to the formation of the Christian philanthropic societies.

The Church celebrates the feast day of St. Basil on January 1, the date on which he fell asleep in the Lord in A.D. 379. Since this date coincides with the first day of the new year, this holiday is especially meaningful for Orthodox Christians.

St. Sylvester, Pope of Rome

Before Christianity was to become the official religion of the civilized world, over three hundred years were to pass after the resurrection of Jesus Christ. The instrument of God who helped to bring about the recognition of the Christian religion was Sylvester, Bishop of Rome.

To understand the concept of papal authority, we must consider the ranks of the priestly orders. There are three spiritual stages or ranks of clergy: the diaconate, in which a candidate is ordained a deacon; the presbytery, in which he is ordained a priest; and the episcopacy, in which a priest is ordained a bishop. The third and highest order embraces celibates worthy to become bishops, then archbishops, metropolitans, and finally patriarchs or popes. Taken from the Greek word *papas*, or spiritual father, the title 'pope' is given to those bishops whose service covered large metropolitan centers such as Alexandria, Constantinople, and Rome.

When we consider that the great majority of the saints of the Christian Church were of humble station and were nearly always martyred in agony, Pope Sylvester's high stature was perhaps an obstacle to his elevation to the company of the saints. Thus, he became a saint in spite of being a pope, and not because of it.

Ordained as bishop at the age of thirty, Sylvester became pope after the death of Pope Miltiades in A.D. 314. This was during the reign of Constantine the Great, who founded the Byzantine Empire in A.D. 324, whose capital Byzantium on the Bosporus became Constantinople.

When Constantine came to power, however, he was not a Christian, but a pagan. Unlike many of his predecessors, he did not condone the persecution of Christians, a practice so fierce and so intense that Christians were often forced to take to the hills and dwell in caves.

As champion of the Christian cause, Sylvester took to the hills himself, rallying his people to a renewed faith in Jesus Christ. His fame spread throughout the land as a tireless man of God, and through his pious work the ranks of Christians greatly increased. Such was his fervor in the name of Christ that he was revered and respected by pagans and Christians alike.

It was his fame that was responsible for the creation of a beautiful legend regarding his encounter with Constantine. According to this story, Emperor Constantine had fallen seriously ill. The high priests of the Temple of Zeus vainly ministered to the ailing monarch; his malady baffled the court physicians. Finally, when all seemed hopeless, the great Christian leader was summoned to the side of the Emperor. In what must have been one of the most dramatic moments in history, the Bishop of Rome stood before the stricken ruler as he lay helpless. He prayed to God for the sick man's recovery and God answered his prayer.

History, however, does tell us that Constantine's interest in the Christian faith increased as time went on. He did see Christ in a vision holding a banner on which was a cross and an inscription reading, "In this sign conquer." Constantine was baptized before he died.

Meanwhile, Pope Sylvester continued to preach faith in Jesus Christ and witnessed the decline of paganism in the civilized world. Just eleven years after the founding of the Byzantine Empire, unlike other saints whose end came violently, Sylvester died peacefully on 2 January 335.

Δ. Δукаƒ

January 2

St. Zorzis (George)
Of Mytelene (Neomartyr)

The feast day of St. Zorzis falls upon the same day as that of Pope Sylvester, even though the two were separated not only by a time span of more than 1400 years, but also by a wide gap in social standing. While Sylvester gloried in the exalted role of pope, Zorzis lived in the ignominy of slavery. That the Church honors on the same day one who lived in reverence while the other lived in wretchedness is further evidence that all men are equal in the sight of God.

During the 400 years under Turkish conquest, Orthodox Christians in general and Greeks in particular suffered untold hardships and persecution at the hands of the unrelenting Ottoman foe, whose Muslim fanaticism defiled the churches of Christ and wreaked every form of misery that could be devised. The survival of Orthodoxy is a tribute to the Christian courage of the Greeks and other Orthodox people. Among the courageous was Zorzis, whose little-known life story epitomized the invincible Christian.

Born and baptized in the Orthodox Faith, Zorzis was a mere lad of twelve and already a devout Christian when his captors sold him into slavery in 1710. His master's Muslim faith was intense; his hatred for Christians was equally so. Exactly what transpired between Zorzis and his master is not known, but it is speculated that they came to respect each other's devotion to his faith, while at the same time not openly admitting it. The strange circumstances under which the boy appeared to have adopted the Muslim faith and language remain a mystery.

During the sixty years of his slavery, the relationship between master and servant was such that Zorzis never sought to embarrass his master. That he continued to serve Christ is unquestionable and how he reconciled his true Christian faith and his apparent adoption of Islam became manifest upon the death of his master. Now that his obligation to his master was ended after sixty long years of enslaved service, his true service to God and Christ was his only obligation. He came forth to openly declare his faith in Christ, stating simply: "I was born an Orthodox Christian and now am prepared to die as an Orthodox Christian—not a Muslim."

The enraged Turks brought him before the magistrate, declaring that he had made a mockery of the Muslims for sixty years by secretly worshipping Christ while feigning Muslim observances. His accusers railed at Zorzis, but he did not flinch. The Greek, who for sixty years had endured in quiet acquiescence, now stood in staunch defiance of his captors.

Unable to accept this defiance as anything but false bravado in the light of sixty years of obeisance, the Turks unleashed their fury by casting Zorzis into a dungeon and thereafter torturing him for days. The will of this Christian was never broken; Zorzis never wavered. To the end denouncing the Muslims and refusing to deny his Christian faith, Zorzis was put to death on 2 January 1770.

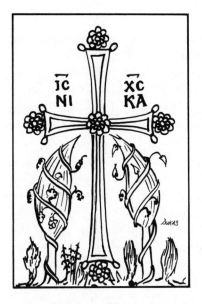

St. Romanos of Karpenisi

The flame of Christianity burns brightly in all corners of the globe: in churches and cathedrals, chapels and shrines. Nowhere does the flame of truth shine more brightly than in the ancient monasteries of Orthodoxy, which for centuries have been spiritual lighthouses beaming the approach to the gates of heaven. Manned by the ranks of holy men—the monks— monasteries have served as bastions of Christianity for hundreds of years. Their mightiest citadel remains Mt. Athos, whose rugged terrain symbolizes the strength of Christianity.

It is said that this holy place was founded through a miracle of the Blessed Virgin Mary. Be that as it may, the lofty promontory of Mt. Athos, which is comprised of 140 square miles of awesome Macedonian coastline, is the site of twenty monasteries of such grandeur and impressiveness that they form a miracle in themselves. This massive array of fortresses is occupied by Christian soldiers from whose ranks have come philosophers, bishops, archbishops, and patriarchs. Mt. Athos has also produced saints, one of whom was Romanos of Karpenisi.

Romanos toiled unceasingly in the works of the Lord during his apprenticeship on Mt. Athos. Because he did not have the benefit of high intellect, scholarly brilliance, or depth of philosophic perception which many other monks possessed, he had to work especially hard. Nevertheless, what he lacked in erudition he more than compensated for in intensity of purpose and complete dedication. He was later led to the Holy Land. When he returned to Mt. Athos, he had become a learned and erudite servant of God. He then completed his spiritual training under the abbot of Kafsokalyvi, Monk Akakios. It was not long before

Romanos, consumed by the spirit of Christianity, commanded the respect of those with whom he walked and worked in the vineyard of the Lord. When alone, he walked with God.

It is not exactly known which of the many sketes—small caves or huts where the monks prayed in solitude—he chose to make his home. There he meditated and prayed to God in a solitude which lent proximity to God. If his skete were known, it would surely be a shrine. However, the saintliness of Romanos and so many of his spiritual brothers of Mt. Athos has been such that the entire peninsula can be considered a special holy place. No visitor has ever gone to Mt. Athos without having enriched his soul and without leaving with an indelible impression and inspiration which he would remember throughout his lifetime. It is truly an oasis of Christianity without equal in all the world.

Romanos lived in the seventeenth century, a time in which the Turkish conquest of Greece had almost annihilated ancient Greek civilization and had defiled Christianity in every manner. The arrogant and ruthless conqueror preyed upon the Christian faithful. They especially persecuted the more outstanding followers of Christ such as Romanos of Karpenisi.

Romanos later left the comparative safety of Mt. Athos to lend his presence in Constantinople, where he encouraged the Christian people and gave them hope in Christ during the Turkish oppression. In 1694, while engaged in God's work in the ancient Byzantine capital, Romanos was apprehended by Turks. After a number of ceremonious gestures, they declared him to be a traitor, a crime for which this innocent and holy man was beheaded. Romanos lives on in the spiritual splendor of Mt. Athos, and he is remembered by the Church on January 5.

SAINT OF
GREGORY NYSSA

D.AUKAS

St. Gregory of Nyssa

Christianity has faced serious crises which menaced its very existence. The most critical threats to our faith arose during the first few centuries of ecclesiastical history. One such crisis developed in the fourth century when the doctrine of Arianism undermined the unity of Orthodoxy as no other doctrine before or since. Among the voices that were raised against the heresy of Arius, none was more eloquent nor more convincing than that of Gregory of Nyssa. Although Christendom has since splintered, the true faith of the Orthodox Church has been preserved intact thanks largely to men such as St. Gregory.

Gregory was a member of the family that boasted of such heroic figures as his brother St. Basil the Great, another brother Peter, Archbishop of Sebastia, and his sister Macrina, the nun whose feast day is July 19. Born in Cappadocia, Asia Minor, Gregory travelled to all the corners of the Empire on triumphant lecturing tours, accompanied by his lovely wife, Theosebia. It was not until his wife's untimely death, however, that Gregory devoted his energies exclusively as a standard bearer of the Orthodox Christian faith. He was ordained Bishop of Nyssa and in that capacity he served with a distinction that was to bring him prominence as an intellectual and religious leader.

The heretical movement of Arius, a theologian and priest of Alexandria, shook the foundations of the Christian faith by claiming that Christ was not the true God, but that he was a man, created by God the Father. Since he was created by the Father, according to Arius, Christ was not equal to the Father, but was lower, subordinate to Him. In this way, the followers of Arius undermined the doctrines of the Holy Trinity and of salvation through Jesus Christ, the God-man. Gregory of Nyssa was instrumental in combatting the false doctrine of Arius.

When the Emperor Valens, an Arian, came to power in A.D. 374, he forthwith banished Gregory who had gone to Constantinople to speak out against the heretical movement. His exile was not long, however. The Emperor Valens, in an ill-considered campaign against invaders streaming in from the Balkans, ordered an attack in which he and his entire army were slaughtered.

After the the death of Valens, Gregory returned to his post at Nyssa and became part of the noble triumvirate with Basil the Great and Gregory Nazianzos, which was greatly responsible for the defeat of Arianism and other heresies. The Second Ecumenical Council (Constantinople, A.D. 381) completed the Nicene Creed as we know it today. The most eloquent voice of the Second Council has generally been accepted to be that of Gregory, Bishop of Nyssa.

Thus, Orthodoxy has withstood the ravages of dissension over a period of nearly two thousand years—a tribute to Christianity itself, to the Orthodox faithful, and to men such as St. Gregory of Nyssa who have come forward in time of crisis to meet the challenge.

St. Gregory died most probably in the year 394 and his memory is commemorated on January 10.

January 13

St. Maximos (Kafsokalyvis)

The incredible saga of the monasteries of Mt. Athos is the summation of the life's work of some of the most noble spirits of Christianity. Among the many holy men of Mt. Athos whose affinity to God has led to their sainthood, perhaps the most noteworthy and certainly the most unique was Maximos, a man whose asceticism and peculiar lifestyle set him apart from his peers. A confirmed non-conformist, Maximos epitomized the rugged individualism of the monks whose behavior was generally considered eccentric by the outside world. Sensual society that deemed monasticism irregular at best would have undoubtedly seen Maximos as hopelessly deranged. And yet, if they had seen his pure spirit they would have knelt before him.

Admitted to the sacred confines of Mt. Athos at the age of seventeen, Maximos, over a span of nearly eighty years, evinced a piety and wisdom that endeared him to countless pilgrims seeking his counsel and blessing. He never ceased to inspire those about him. Although decline had set in on Athos after it was plundered in the thirteenth century during the Fourth Crusade, a revival occurred during the following century. Maximos, part of the revival, along with such stalwarts as St. Gregory Palamas, upheld the doctrine of hesychasm. In fact, he carried hesychasm to the extreme that became his trademark.

Maximos availed himself of the vastness of the Athos peninsula—a promontory stretching thirty miles out into the Aegean Sea, with a width in excess of six miles. When he found it impossible to communicate with God in the monasteries, even in any of the sketes or caves, he fashioned a rude hut in which to meditate and pray. When the hut seemed no longer impervious to anything but purity, he would burn it and build another. This habit caused him to be dubbed Maximos Kafsokalyvis (hut-burner). Living in his hut enveloped in prayer, Maximos thus experienced a greater form of self-denial than simply the solitude and austerity of an anchorite.

Just as Moses had gone up to Mt. Sinai and Elijah to Mt. Carmel, Maximos ascended the holy mountain of Athos—which rises abruptly out of the Aegean for nearly seven thousand feet—an ascent which few have dared to venture. Heedless to the dangers and the biting cold, he scaled the lofty peak, and in the stark seclusion that can be found only on a mountain top, he prostrated himself before the Lord. After a week passed, a vision of the Virgin Mary appeared to him. The Theotokos told Maximos that he would henceforth know spiritual perfection through the Holy Spirit.

Maximos descended the sacred mountain with the wisdom of ages stored within him, and with the sweet serenity of the Holy Spirit in his heart. It was as though he had been reborn, glowing with a presence that suggested an intimacy with the Divine. Word of his transformation brought scores seeking his blessing and healing through the Holy Spirit. As a result, he was so beseiged that he sought the refuge of his dismal hut.

Maximos withdrew to the seclusion of his hut and would have lived out his days there, but he was prevailed upon to grace the community with his presence. Instrumental in drawing him out of seclusion was a noted hermit, Gregory of Sinai, who like many others had gone to Mt. Athos for the express purpose of seeing the holy Maximos.

Mt. Athos contains many miracle-working icons and in the fourteenth century, Maximos was a living icon. This gentle link with divinity lived to be ninety-five years old. Even after his death he continued to serve those of the faithful seeking comfort at his grave site. The fires of his huts have long since gone out, but the flame of his holy spirit will never be extinguished. The Church remembers St. Maximos Kafsokalyvis on January 13.

Δ. Δukaς

January 14

St. Savvas, the Serbian Prince

It was during the thirteenth century that Savvas, son of King Simeon of Serbia and heir to the royal throne, forsook the glory and power of the throne to dedicate himself to the Savior. One of three brothers, Savvas was trained and educated to be a monarch. However, with all due respect for his royal responsibilities, Savvas considered service to the Church to be of greater importance. Since either of his two brothers could assume the throne, he felt free to serve Christ. Later he did not regret his decision to serve the King of Kings.

Savvas was not certain how he could best serve the Church. He above all wanted no special favor because of his royal position. It happened that some monks from Mt. Athos arrived in Serbia to solicit funds from King Simeon. Simeon had been charitable in the past, but on this occasion he gave not only his money, but also his son. Savvas secretly planned to go to Mt. Athos with the monks in order to himself become a monk. He persuaded the monks to take him without his father's knowledge. Savvas argued that he was not betraying his father, but that were he to be denied permission to accompany them, they would be betraying the Lord whom he desperately sought to serve.

Savvas faded into the obscurity of Mt. Athos among the thousands of monks who enjoyed not only spiritual freedom, but total independence from the state without fear of intervention. After being tonsured a monk, Savvas soon established himself in the brotherhood as a man of great intelligence and profound devotion to the word of the Lord.

Meanwhile King Simeon had instituted a broad search for his son. Two years after Savvas' secret departure, the hunt came to an end with the revelation that he had left of his own volition to become an ascetic. Although the King's emissaries advised Savvas his only course of action was to return to his rightful place at the side of his father, Savvas sent them back with a letter for his parents. In his letter, which was reputed to have been four hundred pages long, Savvas not only extolled the virtues and importance of monasticism, but in a torrent of passionate prose he also revealed to them the true meaning of Christian love and the depth of his devotion to Jesus Christ.

Greatly moved by his son's impassioned letter, the King transferred the royal authority to his two sons and then journeyed to Mt. Athos to experience first-hand what had been so eloquently described to him. Shedding the royal purple for a monk's habit, the King found for himself a serenity he had never known before. Soon many of his countrymen joined him and his son, eventually founding Chilandarion, the first Serbian monastery on Mt. Athos.

Impressed by the holy work of Savvas, the Patriarch of Constantinople prevailed upon him to return to his native Serbia to serve his people not as king, but as archbishop of Serbia. With considerable reluctance Savvas left Mt. Athos to respect the patriarch's wishes and assume the spiritual leadership of his native land. His service was one of distinction; the Orthodox Church of Serbia flourished as never before in its history. Savvas eventually returned to his beloved Chilandarion where he died peacefully on 14 January 1236.

St. Anthony the Great

The Council of Nicaea, convened by the Emperor Constantine in A.D. 325, was attended by the most important leaders of Christianity from all corners of the Roman Empire. Second in importance to no other council in Church history, this Council was called to answer many crucial questions of theology and dogma. Among the issues discussed was the highly controversial doctrine of the Alexandrian priest Arius, who questioned the divinity of Jesus Christ. The Arian doctrine concerning the relationship of Christ to God the Father was vigorously denounced by the leading prelates as heresy. Among those who spoke in opposition to the Arian heresy was the saintly monk Anthony. His eloquent defense of the Orthodox belief in Christ as true God earned him the title of St. Anthony the Great.

Anthony was born of extremely humble parents in the year A.D. 251 in Coma in middle Egypt. He received no education and when he was orphaned at eighteen he had not yet learned to read and write. In spite of this handicap he sought to learn the meaning of his existence. One day he was greatly impressed by a sermon based on a text from St. Matthew in which Christ said: "If you would be perfect, go, sell what you possess and give to the poor, and you will have treasure in heaven; and come and follow me." Anthony then sold his meager belongings, gave the money to the poor, and went into the Egyptian desert. There he met a group of monks who took him into their care.

In the desert Anthony applied himself diligently to prayer and study. Before he had mastered reading and writing, he is said to have committed to memory several passages from the

Bible just by listening to the monks reading to him. Following a period of many years of self-denial, during which he not only acquired a scholarly intimacy with the Scriptures but also a proximity to God, he emerged as a man of piety. As a result, his counsel was sought by both monks and laymen.

When the Council of Nicaea was convened, Anthony was seventy-four years old and was recognized as a man whose wisdom commanded respect. For this reason he was invited to attend this historic meeting despite the fact that he held neither title nor power. His eloquent defense of the Orthodox doctrine concerning the person of Jesus Christ was instrumental in weakening the position of Arianism. His witness led to the eventual and complete elimination of Arianism.

Returning to his Egyptian desert monastery, St. Anthony applied himself to refining the rules of monasticism and to establishing a chain of monasteries. He attracted hundreds of monks to asceticism and greatly furthered the propagation of the Christian faith. Anthony's inspired leadership led to the creation of a monasticism in which active participation in the spread of Christianity was fostered through writing and counseling. At the same time this form of monasticism did not neglect private meditation and prayer.

The monastic rules of St. Anthony, the 'patriarch' of monastic life have served as the basis for countless monasteries. The years of hardship he endured in the desert belie the guidelines set today for longevity; St. Anthony lived to the age of 105. He died in his desert retreat in A.D. 356. St. Anthony, whose name is synonymous with a monasticism of devotion and vigor, is honored on January 17.

S A I N T

Δ. Δυκας

A T H A N A S I O S

January 18 (also May 2)

St. Athanasios

Although St. Athanasios was, according to English historian Gibbon, author of the classic *Decline and Fall of the Roman Empire,* more capable of ruling the Roman Empire than all of the sons of Constantine, nevertheless for all his greatness he remained one of the most tragic figures of the early Christian era. Of small stature and boundless vigor, Athanasios rose to prominence in the hierarchy, yet remained at heart an unworldly and unyielding monk. He was at the center of religious strife in a critical period of early Christianity and was in and out of favor with the emperors in perhaps the stormiest career of any clergyman.

Born in Alexandria, Egypt, in A.D. 297, Athanasios was associated with the Alexandrian chancery at an early age, having been ordained deacon in the year 319 and subsequently priest. His brilliance was shown in his "Sermon Against the Arians", written to answer the widely spreading heresy of Arianism which had been condemned in 318 by a local synod. According to Arius, an elderly priest of Alexandria, Father, Son, and Holy Spirit were three separate essences or substances, which is contrary to Orthodox teaching. The spread of Arianism prompted Emperor Constantine to convene the First Ecumenical Council in Nicaea (A.D. 325), where Athanasios brilliantly opposed the false doctrine of Arius. Nevertheless, the controversy was to last for another two centuries. The conciliatory tone of the Council of Nicaea was not enough to put an end to the heresy; Arius would not comply with its decisions and thus fled to Palestine.

At the age of thirty Athanasios was made Bishop of Alexandria. Although Arius assured the Emperor that he accepted the creed of Nicaea, the suspicious Athanasios defied the imperial order for Arius' reinstatement. For this he was banished, taking refuge in Treves, France, the place of his first exile, from which he returned in 337 after Constantine's death. The same year though, his enemies conspired to have him again banished by a synod in Antioch. Athanasios, eluding those who would have him imprisoned, traveled to Rome to plead his case before the Pope, Julius I. Although a council at Sardica favored Athanasios, he did not return from exile until 345, after the death of usurper Bishop Gregory.

Once again his enemies sprang into action and at a council in Milan in 355, Athanasios was deposed. Thus, after ten years of fruitful rule, he took refuge with the monks of the Egyptian desert whom he greatly admired and whom he had befriended. While with the monks he wrote the *History of the Arian Heresy,* which displays his vehemence and ironic humor.

In 361 Athanasios was again restored as Bishop of Alexandria and immediately resumed his struggle against Arianism. After a series of lengthy and complicated discussions, councils, synods, and other forums of debate, a credal formula was adopted which satisfied those whose middle view led them to be called Semi-Arians. Peace had hardly arrived when another storm came in the form of the regeneration of paganism under the Emperor Julian the Apostate. In the autumn of 363, Athanasios was again put to flight, only to return a short time later, after the death of the Emperor. He enjoyed a comparative calm until he was removed by Emperor Valens during another resurgence of paganism. Four months later, the aging bishop was recalled and allowed to live out his life in comparative peace.

Greatly admired by the Orthodox and hated by the heretics he so adamantly opposed, Athanasios stirred the emotions of the Christians as perhaps no other Father of the Church. His theological doctrine is clear and uncomplicated in the strictest Orthodox tradition, and his encouragement of monasticism was a labor of love. He died 2 May 373.

January 19

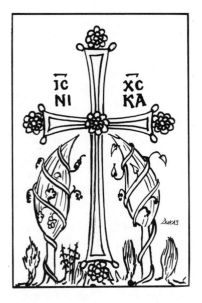

St. Mark of Ephesos

Early in the fifteenth century, the incursions of the Ottoman Turkish forces into the Byzantine Empire menaced the very existence of Christianity. Indeed, Orthodox Christianity in the Balkans and the Middle East might very well have lost its identity but for the efforts of its stalwarts, chief among whom was Mark of Ephesos. Although Orthodoxy owes a debt of gratitude to many devout and brave souls who helped to preserve her ancient faith, deepest thanks must be reserved for St. Mark.

Scion of a distinquished family, Mark was born in the year 1392 of a lineage which promised him prominence from the moment of his birth. His father served with distinction in the imperial government and his mother was the daughter of one of Constantinople's outstanding physicians. The family honor and tradition were carried out by Mark, but on the higher plateau he chose to live and work for the glory of God and His Son. Displaying rare brilliance of mind and profound religious conviction, he ascended the ladder of religious leadership and was elevated to the post of Metropolitan of Ephesos, a prestigious spiritual center of Orthodoxy. Among his accomplishments was an impressive series of writings on church affairs which for insight, perceptiveness, and devotion may have been equalled but never surpassed.

At this time the Turkish threat was very great: the borders of the empire were being systematically reduced by the invaders who, in fact, were within striking distance of the Byzantine capital. The Orthodox Church was thus compelled to seek assistance from the Pope of Rome, whose army of trained mercenaries would, they hoped, provide the much needed military support. In response to this appeal, Rome convoked a council in the cities of Ferrara and Florence. Representatives from all over Orthodoxy, including the Orthodox of Russia, the Holy Land, and the Ecumenical Patriarchate, were in attendance. The two great figures of Eastern Christendom, Emperor John VIII and Patriarch Joseph of Constantinople, had travelled to Ferrara for the council and had brought with them the Church's most eloquent defender, Mark of Ephesos.

The meetings were to extend for months, from 1438 to 1439, primarily due to an impasse stemming from the Pope's insistence that no military assistance would be forthcoming unless the Orthodox Church agreed to a unity with Rome under the papal stipulation. This thinly disguised extortion no doubt contributed to the death of the disillusioned Patriarch Joseph, which in turn threw the meetings into greater turmoil. The pressure to submit to Rome was so great that in a unilateral gesture the Russian Orthodox representatives signed the articles of unity and were joined by splinter groups of Orthodox faithful who feared the invader more than Rome.

Mark of Ephesos, however, staunchly refused to submit to Rome. Storming out of the council in protest, he vowed never to submit to what he thought was little other than tyranny. He returned to Ephesos to lead a movement against so-called unity which Rome contrived. Mark firmly upheld the purity of the Orthodox faith which had not yielded to any external influence since the time of Christ. He was instrumental in rallying the faithful to a clear defiance of papal pressure and a reaffirmation of Orthodox principles. Subsequent events saw the failure of this infamous attempt for unity, the exile of the Russian metropolitan, and the return of those who had strayed from the Orthodox faith. In a time when Orthodoxy sorely needed a show of spiritual fortitude, Mark of Ephesos scorned the mailed fist. For this he was banished by the Emperor, whose concern for his city was greater than his concern for the purity of Orthodoxy. After two years of banishment, Mark of Ephesos returned to great acclaim in Constantinople where he died in 1444.

January 21st

St. Neophytos

The ancient Greeks were looking in the right direction
when they gazed toward the
summit of lofty Mount Olympos as the dwelling place of
their gods; but for centuries
the focus of the Greeks was
short. It was the Apostles of
Christ who extended their
sight to the Kingdom of
Heaven. Not long after St. Paul's appearance on Mars Hill before a gathering of the Athenians, Zeus and his fellow gods
were supplanted by human beings who literally dwelled on the
mountain, tranquilly searching for the company of God through
the power of Jesus Christ. Three hundred years after the
appearance of Christ, Mt. Olympos was transformed from the
campsite of imaginary supernaturals to the quiet abode of
pious monks.

The Olympic slopes came to be occupied by many pious men,
monks, hermits, and prelates, whose combined spiritual efforts
were to glorify the Christian religion. In some instances,
miracles were worked through the Holy Spirit. While it never
achieved the spiritual status of Mt. Athos, Mt. Olympos nevertheless did produce some extraordinary figures of Christendom, among whom was the little-known Neophytos.

Neophytos was born into a society of early Christians whose
depth of faith and whose sacrifices were of such magnitude that
it is little wonder that all Christians of the first three centuries
were not recognized as saints. The quiet courage of Neophytos
in the face of unspeakable horror set the example for his con-
temporaries in their unshakable faith.

Under circumstances which would have discouraged one of
weaker will, Neophytos enthusiastically accepted the word

of Christ at an early age. Although Christians were cruelly persecuted at that time, he pursued the happiness of the Christian religion with undiminishing zeal. From very early youth he participated in the church services which the faithful held underground to escape their persecutors. He grew to fully comprehend the word of God and the truth of Jesus Christ. One day an angel of the Lord appeared in a vision to the parents of the young Neophytos and advised them that their son would be called to the service of God. The very next day Neophytos approached his parents and said that he felt he should enter the monastic life to find God.

Neophytos chose the heights of Olympos, some 10,000 feet above sea level, as his new dwelling place. When not in the company of the many monks who sought sanctuary there, he lived in a skete of his own where he strove to attain the "perfect life" through piety, asceticism, prayer, and meditation. His commitment to God was total, yet never did he lose sight of his responsibility to his fellow Christians, whom he served with care and devotion. While reading the Scriptures one day, he was visited by a holy messenger who informed him that his parents were ailing and near death. Ignoring the fact that the most coveted prey of the pagans was a holy man of Mt. Olympos, he hastened to his parents in the city of Nicaea, comforting them until each had passed on.

The watchful eye of a centurion brought the gentle Neophytos to trial and swift punishment for his Christianity. When Neophytos refused to disavow Christ and worship the pagan idols, he was subjected to inhuman tortures. Afterwards he was thrown into an arena in which the wild animals refused to attack him. Neophytos earned the martyr's crown when a soldier's lance ended his earthly life on January 21.

Δ. Δυκας

St. Timothy

To a man called Timothy fell the solemn honor of being the recipient of two letters from the great Apostle St. Paul, who wrote these sacred epistles in his final hours before his martyrdom, while a captive of Nero. Now known as the Pastoral Epistles, they are the two books of the New Testament entitled First Timothy and Second Timothy. In them are set forth the regulations for all aspects of Church worship and a bestowal of apostolic trust upon a young man whom St. Paul chose to "labor and suffer reproach" in spreading the word of Christ, and whom St. Paul embraced as a son.

He was born in Lystra in Lyconia of a pagan Greek father and a Jewish mother named Eunice. His grandmother was a Christian and it was perhaps through her influence and teaching that he came to follow Christ. When the Apostle Paul visited Lystra, the young Timothy was already a full member of the Christian Church and after the two discussed the many difficulties Christianity was facing, the younger man expressed a desire to serve as a missionary, despite its hazards. It was after the departure of Barnabus and Mark that Paul summoned Timothy to accompany him as a colleague in the cause of Christ.

About a quarter of a century after Christ had died, Timothy and Paul traveled to Europe, accompanied by Silas, in a missionary task of staggering proportion. In most areas theirs was at best a thankless job, but with the zeal born of a profound love of the Savior they succeeded in securing a foothold in spiritually darkened corners. They brought this about with administrative skill in the face of odds which might have discouraged less hardy souls. In a fury of religious oratory, they_ summoned thousands to the fold and established churches of God where for centuries people had worshipped mere objects or beasts out of fear and superstition.

When Paul was summoned to Athens, he commissioned Timothy to carry the word of Christ to Corinth, Thessaloniki, and Phillipi. To these areas Timothy displayed his talents to the fullest in establishing a nucleus of Christian churches which became the cornerstone from which Christianity has grown to its present day proportions. With the help of subordinate apostles he instilled in the populace a love of the Savior. Under his leadership Churches were built, the form of worship was set forth, and capable ministry for all services was established.

Overcoming obstacles strewn in his missionary path, Timothy made his way to Ephesos. There he was established as Bishop and took on the formidable task of putting Christ into the hearts of people who lived in fear and awe of the pagan god Artemis. This was a god to be reckoned with because of its alleged powers and because it was said to have made its home in Ephesos, much as Olympos was the home of Zeus and his cohorts. Timothy was more than equal to the challenge of supplanting this symbol of darkness with the light of Jesus. In the eyes of the people, his successful establishment of Christianity in Ephesos was equivalent to driving the lion from its den.

This true man of God opposed the terrorists who profaned religion with their quarrelsome and self-seeking orgies performed for Artemis. The pagans grew more and more resentful of the presence of Timothy and out of their hatred evolved an aura of terror. One evening, when one of their eerie rituals had spilled out into the streets and had carried them out in front of the Church of Christ, Timothy emerged to denounce them, whereupon the frenzied mob stoned him to death. Timothy died a martyr for Christ on 22 January 72.

SAINT GREGORY THE THEOLOGIAN

D. Dukas

St. Gregory the Theologian

Of the twenty centuries since the birth of Christ no single century has had crowded into it so many great events as the fourth century, which witnessed a fragmented Christendom pieced together by men of God. Were it not for the efforts of such men, Christianity would not have become the spiritual haven of mankind it is today. The fabric of Christendom was woven into its strength and beauty of character by the threads of men such as St. Gregory the Theologian, who became one of the four great doctors of the Church during this era, along with Basil the Great, John Chrysostom and Athanasios the Great. He is further remembered as one of the three so-called Cappadocian Fathers, an honor he shares with Basil and Gregory of Nyssa. He is also recognized as the champion of Orthodoxy against the heretical doctrine of Arianism.

The son of a bishop for whom he was named, Gregory was born in Nazianzos in Cappadocia, Asia Minor, in 329. He was educated in Caesaria and then in Athens, where he met Basil and became close friends linked in a common resolve to serve Christ. At the suggestion of Basil the two friends became monastics at a retreat in Pontios, where each embarked on a spiritual journey that was to lead them both to greatness. It was with some degree of reluctance, however, that Gregory left the monastery to be ordained into the priesthood to serve as an assistant to his father, the Bishop of Nazianzos. The son's brilliance as a preacher outshone his father's. When barely 30 years old he won acclaim throughout the region as a mighty warrior in the fight against paganism and heresy.

It was largely through the influence of Gregory that his friend Basil was made Bishop of Caesaria. In the process he himself was made bishop of the relatively unimportant town of Sasima, a post he never sought and in which he never served, preferring to remain with his father in Nazianzos. He took over the church of Nazianzos after the death of his father in 374. With the loss of his father he had a longing to return to asceticism in some retreat, there to meditate, pray, and interpret the Scriptures. He was allowed to go to the seclusion of Selucia in Isauria, where his tenure as an eremite was short-lived.

After the death of the Arian Emperor Valens, followed closely by the death of his friend Basil, Gregory was called to Constantinople. He was to head the reorganization of the Orthodox Church which had been torn asunder by the heresy of Arianism from within and by the harassment of pagans without. In the course of this holy work, he achieved distinction as orator, traditionalist, and crusader that earned him the title of "theologos" despite the opposition of Maximos the Cynic, who had been set up against him by the Bishop of Alexandria.

When the Orthodox Emperor Theodosios came to power in 380, Gregory assumed the direction of the magnificent Church of Haghia Sophia, the most prestigious house of God in all Christendom. While director of this mighty church, Gregory took part in a council held in Constantinople in 381 to settle the differences among the prelates of the Church. Known as the Second Ecumenical Council, it resolved the issues and voted to accept Gregory as Patriarch of Constantinople. It further added its official support to the Nicene doctrine which was championed at the First Council.

For as long as he held the post of spiritual leader of Orthodoxy the gallant Gregory served with honor and dignity. Moreover, he was the instrument of God in unifying the Church into a cohesive unit that could withstand any internal or external pressure. He grew weary of the personal attacks that are the occupational hazard of a patriarch and after a moving farewell address, he retired to live out his days in meditation, writing, and prayer. He died 25 January 388.

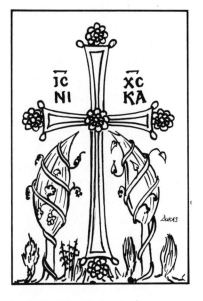

January 28th

St. Ephraim the Syrian

One saint whose holiness of life was recognized unanimously by every sector of Christendom was a humble Syrian named Ephraim. He is revered not only by the Orthodox Church, but also by the Roman Catholic and the Eastern Rite of Syria as well. Although he was born in Syria in A.D. 306 Ephraim's impact on the Christian religion was such that sixteeen centuries later, in 1920, Pope Benedict XV decreed that this pious Syrian be listed among the "Fathers of the Church." This is a distinction which is reserved for the most deserving of the untold numbers who have toiled in the service of Christ. This unheralded and relatively unknown saint left a legacy of prose and lyrical hymns which are treasured by the Orthodox Church. Ephraim's prayers and hymns are as much a part of the worship of the Church as the icons themselves are.

Although Ephraim's father was reported to have been a pagan priest, he evidently did not object when Ephraim's mother embraced the Christian faith. Thus, even though his father was a pagan priest, Ephraim was raised a Christian. In spite of this difficult and sometimes embarrassing situation, Ephraim became completely absorbed in the study of the Christian faith with such dedication and objectivity as to place him among the fathers of Christianity.

The intellectual powers of Ephraim came to the fore when he was a student of Bishop Iakovos, a teacher with considerable influence in the city of Nisibus, Syria. Bishop Iakovos delighted in the literary and musical talent of his gifted pupil and fellow Syrian and greatly encouraged him. After intensive study of all fields of knowledge, including philosophy, theology, and hymnology, Ephraim turned to creative efforts in literature and music. These established him as one of the most gifted and prolific contributors to sacred expression in the annals of the Christian Church. Not one to stray from his high purpose, Ephraim did not turn from his creative work in order to acquire a mastery of other languages. As a result all his masterful dissertations and beautiful hymns had to be translated from the Syrian tongue.

Tonsured as a monk by his friend and confidant, Bishop Iakovos, he was eventually ordained a deacon. Despite this prominence in Church affairs, he chose no advancement in the hierarchy, preferring the monastic life which afforded him greater opportunity to express himself in word and in song.

Ephraim was reported to have attended the First Ecumenical Council in Nicaea (A.D. 325) with Bishop Iakovos. Later he became director of a Syrian theological school, where his genius as teacher, lecturer, writer, and hymnographer earned him a world-wide reputation. When the persecution of Christians intensified in A.D. 363, he was forced to seek refuge in the community of Edessa on the banks of the Euphrates. There he continued to develop his creative talents to the glory of God and consequently the people of Edessa referred to him as "the lyre of the Holy Spirit."

Throughout his lifetime Ephraim continued to write works of poetic beauty in which he expressed his Christian faith. Furthermore, according to St. Gregory of Nyssa, Ephraim had "written commentaries on the Old and New Testament as no other Father of the Church with such insight and wisdom." Among those who concurred with this opinion was St. Gregory's brother, St. Basil. In spite of the accolades which he received during his own lifetime for his great accomplishments in Christian expression, Ephraim preferred the simplicity of monasticism, eschewing the pomp and trappings of high office. He died on 28 January 373.

SAINT

ABRAMIOS

Δ. Δukas

February 4th

St. Abramios,
Bishop of Arbela, Persia

Three centuries after the birth of Christ the ancient land of Persia continued to retain its inherent mysticism and conglomeration of religious cults and sects, each of which eyed the other with suspicion but, nevertheless, found a common ground in superstition. What made this strange land stranger still was the fanatic devotion to concepts that eventually spawned such ideas as flying carpets, Alladins and Sinbads. That Christianity took a foothold in such a hostile environment is a tribute to the miraculous strength of Christianity itself. Nevertheless, a sizeable Christian community arose in Persia and became a vital and powerful force, in spite of the hostile environment.

Abramios was named Bishop of Arbela during the reign of Sapur II (371-379). Christian communities continued to establish themselves throughout the land. The spread of Christianity was so great that Bishop Abramios had difficulty keeping pace with the new communities and meeting their needs. He was most successful in winning large areas of the land to the cause of peace in the name of Jesus Christ. In fact, his successive triumphs became the envy of the soothsayers, magicians, and the religous fanatics of the occult. Soon they came to look upon Bishop Abramios as a threat to their own influence. In due course, his enemies bore down on the good bishop with a harsh and unrelenting vengeance.

In a country where treachery and sorcery flourished, it was no great task to bring Bishop Abramios to their own brand of justice. The corrupt rulers, whose authority was in the hands of religious and other demagogues, listened with nodding approval at the grave charges brought against the Christian bishop. When the charges mounted to treason, the judges had no recourse but to cast this very dangerous Christian into prison.

The prisons of ancient Persia not only agonized men's bodies but also tried their very souls. It was in such a prison of ancient Persia that the soft-spoken Christian Bishop Abramios was put to unspeakable torment. Under such dire circumstances one could understand how any man could give in to his tormentors and deny Christ. The unmerciful beatings continued to the point of death, but with cruel cunning he was allowed to recover just enough to absorb more punishment. At each point he was given the opportunity to denounce Christ and worship the sun as the Persians did. Each time the bishop reaffirmed his belief in Christ, the Son of God, who created the sun they saw fit to worship.

When the scimitar of an infuriated Persian severed the head of Bishop Abramios from his battered body on 4 February 347, the soul of Bishop Abramios ascended to Heaven.

February 10

St. Charalambos

The invincibility of Christiannity is epitomized by the superhuman endurance of the priest Charalambos, who suffered inhuman tortures and martyrdom at the hands of pagan tormentors. No single martyr was recorded to have endured as much physical punishment as Charalambos. He was an obscure Orthodox priest who earned his sainthood solely by his steadfastness to the Christian faith in the face of prolonged agonies. Although this seemingly indestructible servant of the Lord had that divine courage and steadfastness of faith which placed him among the saints, he was human and his flesh and blood felt the pain of torture as sharply as any ordinary man. Few Christians have been asked to pledge their allegiance to Christ under interminable cruelty. Charalambos proved faithful to the end. For his steadfast refusal to renounce the Lord, he is venerated as a saint in the highest tradition of the martyr.

Charalambos lived in the town of Magnesia in Asia Minor during the second century. He was ordained a priest at an early age to serve his home town in a province fiercely hostile to Christians. His reputation as a preacher and man of God placed him as the leader of the tiny Christian body that grew steadily under his influence in spite of great odds. A man of the people, Charalambos brought the light of the Lord's love to everyone in his community. In so doing he also brought down upon himself the envy and wrath of those in power.

The provincial governor, Loukianos, had little regard for the welfare of his people; for the Christians he had nothing but utter contempt. A confrontation between the governor and Chara- lambos was inevitable, as was the result of their meeting. After a brief exchange of formalities the governor unequivocally de- clared that Charalambos must renounce Christ or be punished. This set the scene for the longest period of human suffering in the name of the Savior. When he refused to worship the idols, his persecutors began a planned assault on his body. Loukianos unleashed his merciless hatred for Christians.

Charalambos was first lashed to a post in the public square to be held up to public scorn and ridicule. Then they slashed him repeatedly with sharp knives, taking care that no wound would be fatal. When Charalambos refused to denounce the Lord, they cut him down and dragged him through the streets by his beard. He endured the extremely painful grating of his skin by the pebbled surface as well as the merciless kicking of sandaled feet. Finally propping him up on his feet, they de- manded that he renounce Jesus; once again he refused.

All of the various tortures applied to Charalambos are over- shadowed by the cruel fact that he endured them all. After a systematic series of cruelties that spanned several months, the derision of the pagans turned to wonder at the power and the faith of this Christian. When their methods of punishment only served to draw converts to Christianity, Charalambos' enemies sought to put him quickly to death. The local people rose in opposition to his planned death. Charalambos had helped many afflicted people who were brought to him. The matter was brought up before Emperor Servius, who ordered the battered priest to be brought to Antioch, Syria. Once there, Charalambos was led through the streets with a horse's bit in his mouth. Then they nailed him to a cross. Not only did Charalambos refuse to relent, but he also refused to die. Then they ordered him to be beheaded. Just as his executioners were about to carry out the sentence, a voice said, "Well done, my faithful servant; enter into the Kingdom of Heaven." At that moment he died without a blow being struck, thus denying the pagans their revenge. The two executioners were immediately converted. He died for Christ in A.D. 192.

Δ. Δukaf

February 11

St. Theodora the Empress

Anyone bearing the name Theodora must feel an inner pride in having been so named. It not only means the "gift of God," but is also the namesake of one of the most noble souls in all Christianity. Theodora was the wife of Theophilos, Emperor of the Byzantine Empire during the ninth century, when the Empire was at its zenith and encompassed the entire civilized world.

During this period iconoclasm was a strong, swift-moving force which swept the Empire. The supporters of the iconoclastic movement believed that icons should be purged from the church. They thought that veneration of icons was tantamount to idolatry. In fact, many Orthodox Christians had come to believe that icons, rather than being symbolic, were to be worshipped for themselves. As a reaction against this false understanding of the place of icons in Orthodox worship, many favored the complete elimination of icons. Believing that they were fighting against idolatry, some Emperors issued decrees banishing icons from the churches and persecuting anyone possessing icons. Theophilos was such an iconoclast Emperor, but due solely to the efforts of his most noble wife, Theodora, he was the last. After 150 years iconoclasm was finally defeated.

During the reign of her iconoclast husband, Theodora secretly possessed many icons. She would kneel in prayer and meditation before her icons, firm in the belief that the time was at hand when the icons would once again resume their rightful place in the house of God.

Shortly after the death of Emperor Theophilos, one of the first official acts of Empress Theadora as regent for her son Michael III was to reinstate icons. To do this she convoked a General Council in A.D. 843. This Council formally accepted the use of icons in Orthodox worship, affirming that veneration is paid to Christ and the saints depicted on the icons, and not to the material substance of paint and wood. This historic decision is celebrated each year in the Orthodox Church on the first Sunday of Lent, known as the Sunday of Orthodoxy.

Thus Empress Theodora gave all her support to the recognition of icons as essential elements of Orthodox worship, and in so doing proved to be an instrument of God's glory. In her lifetime she revealed her true nature to be more religious than civic, and because of her faith and devotion to Christ, the Church became as mighty as the Empire. With her precious icons before her, she died on 11 February 859, a true champion of the Orthodox faith.

St. Zacharias

Too few Christians are aware of the sainthood of Zacharias. Fewer still know that God chose Zacharias to be the father of St. John the Baptist, the Forerunner of the Savior. In this way, Zacharias was an instrument of God's divine plan for the salvation of man through Jesus Christ. He prepared the way for his son John, who in turn prepared the way of the Lord, Jesus Christ. Thus, the appearance of John, like that of Christ, was no accident of birth, and Zacharias was an instrument of God for this most solemn purpose.

Zacharias served God in the Temple of Jerusalem. Together with his wife Elizabeth, he led a life of piety. They had no children and accepted their childlessness as God's will. Their situation changed, however, when God sent the Archangel Gabriel to Zacharias to tell him that his wife Elizabeth would bear him a son whom he should call John. Because his wife had exceeded the age of childbearing, Zacharias asked that a sign be given. Although Gabriel assured Zacharias that he would indeed become a father, Zacharias still did not believe. Consequently, he was rendered mute as a sign. His speech would not be restored until the Lord so deemed. At the exact moment of the birth of his son John, when Zacharias was enabled to speak, he could but weep for joy.

John was born a few months before Jesus and was similarly an intended victim of King Herod's decree that all children under the age of two should be put to death. By this abominable decree Herod hoped to assure the death of the newborn Savior among the slain infants. When the Holy Family fled to Egypt, Elizabeth took her precious baby to the hills outside of

Jerusalem. Zacharias remained behind to face the wrath of Herod who had been told that this most holy man was the father of a son who had been spirited out of Jerusalem. He tried to appease Herod's wrath to no avail, however, and was told that if he revealed the whereabouts of his offspring he would not be punished. This ludicrous proposition was scornfully spurned, and in due course the harsh justice was meted out and the kindly Zacharias was put to death.

With no next of kin to claim the martyred father, the record of his internment was lost. For centuries he lay in obscurity in an unmarked grave. However, in A.D. 409, during the reign of Emperor Theodosios, Kalimenos, a man about whom nothing is known except his name, fortuitously discovered the burial site of St. John's father. The remains of Zacharias, clad with white vestments, with a gold mitre on his head, and on his feet the golden sandals he had worn in the Temple, were uncovered on 11 February 409. Each year on this day the Church observes the feast day of Zacharias.

February 12

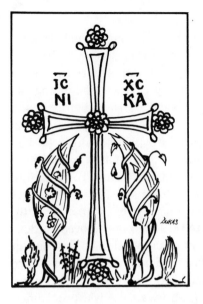

St. Christos, the Gardener

When God created the earth, He saw fit to place man in a garden, the Garden of Eden; ever since the garden has become a symbol of serenity, peace and kinship with God. In what better setting could man live the abundant life promised by the Bible to those who follow Christ than in a garden.

To know nature is to know God. It is largely because of this that the humble gardener Christos acquired intimacy with God which placed him among the saints of Christendom. His talent for tending the living things of the Lord paralleled his ability to attend to the needs of his soul and those of his brethren.

Born in Albania, he found his way to Constantinople where he became the gardener for the Sultan in 1748. Although he was an Orthodox Christian he worked in the garden of the Sultan. Because of this the Muslims envied him greatly. They considered him beneath their station and unworthy to set foot in the Sultan's garden, let alone bear the responsibility of its upkeep.

Unheeding, Christos labored with such diligence that the garden flourished in beauty. His astonishing success with the plant life, which Christos realized was a gift from God, served only to intensify the smoldering envy of those about him. It seemed that the kind and gentle Christos, in nurturing his garden, also nurtured a hatred in others of the Sultan's employ. So intense was their hatred that only the complete destruction of the good gardener could appease their wrath. The gathering storm was evident to Christos, but he knew his faith in God would shelter him.

Those plotting Christos' downfall knew that the only accusation certain to doom Christos was that of treason. His labors were such that he could be forgiven any human fraility. His enemies plotted to draw him into a discussion of his religion, and then bear false witness against him. Their evil scheme was accomplished. Christos was falsely accused of holding the Muslim faith up to ridicule, scorn, and derision before many witnesses.

Consequently, Christos was cast into prison, where he languished for two years under harsh treatment that would have wrenched the soul out of a lesser man. By brutal torture they sought to make Christos recant to save his life. Lashes and chains could not make this man disavow his Christian faith. They promised him the chance to return to his beloved gardens in exchange for a simple statement of conversion to the Muslim faith. Christos remained steadfast. He accepted the sentence of death knowing that his enemies had failed. On 12 February, 1752, he was beheaded. Not long afterward he was proclaimed a martyr and canonized as a neo-martyr, taking his place among the saints of God.

February 12

St. Meletios
(of Antioch, Syria)

The dominating influence in the Byzantine Empire during the eleventh century was the Orthodox faith due to the fact that there was no real separation of powers, no clear-cut separation of Church and State. It followed, therefore, that the Emperors were an accepted power in the Church as well as the State, and that the bishops exerted influence on affairs outside of the Church. The Church and State worked together for the spiritual and general welfare of the people.

It was during the reign of Constantios (4th century), son of Constantine the Great, that there came upon the scene Meletios, a man destined for greatness and for sainthood. While serving his post, Meletios established himself as a man of such great piety and wisdom that when the Patriarchal See of Antioch was vacated, he was unanimously chosen to ascend the patriarchal throne. He was ultimately to prove himself a true man of God in his successful stand against one of the great heresies to ever menace the Church.

This menace was known as Arianism, so called for its principal advocate, Arius, an Egyptian priest. The heretic Arius sowed the vile seed of his philosophy throughout the Middle East and it soon found root in many areas. He held that Jesus Christ, the Son of God, was a created member of the human race and therefore his divinity was open to question. Reasoning that there was only one God and therefore one divinity, the concept of a God-man in one person was not as the Church had long held. The eloquence of the Arians was such that it lured many Bishops of the Antioch area into the fold. Meletios found himself battling against overwhelming odds. Because of his adamant refusal to even consider the new beliefs espoused by the innovators of his time, the worthy bishop was swept from office by a torrent of Arian followers.

The combined forces of Arianism were no match for Meletios. However, he quickly convened the Second Ecumenical Council held in Constantinople in A.D. 381. At this Council Meletios held his position sealing the doom of Arianism. His impassioned arguments for the divinity of Jesus Christ won over even the most stubborn opponents. He vigorously defended the time-honored beliefs of Christianity to the point of exhaustion.

While the deliberations were in progress he ignored his failing health by working ceaselessly toward a unified and viable Church. Before the proceedings had been concluded, Meletios' frail health gave way and he died on 12 February 382, a martyr to the cause of Christianity. His efforts had not been in vain. The doctrine of Arianism was condemned by the Council and Arius was excommunicated; the doctrine of the Holy Trinity was reaffirmed and the memory of Meletios made sacred for all time.

February 13

D. Δukaς

SS. Aquila and Priscilla

There are few saints who are commemorated twice during the Church calendar, but such is the case of Aquila. He is remembered by the Church both singly on July 14 and together with his wife on February 13. The name of Aquila's remarkable wife who attained sainthood with him was Priscilla. Her name is synonymous in ecclesiastical history with piety and Christian zeal of the greatest magnitude.

Born a God-fearing Hebrew in a remote region of the Black Sea, Aquila, together with his equally devout and highly intelligent wife Priscilla, settled in the ancient city of Corinth during the reign of Claudius, Emperor of Rome A.D. 48. Aquila was a tentmaker, a trade which he shared with the great St. Paul. In fact, he met St. Paul in Corinth and this event changed the course of his life as well as that of his wife, Priscilla. After listening to St. Paul, Aquila and Priscilla converted to Christianity. As a matter of fact, St. Paul was so impressed by his new converts that he himself baptized them into the Christian faith. That St. Paul greatly loved them is evidenced by the fact that they were mentioned several times in his epistles (Romans 16.3; Corinthians 16.19; 2 Timothy 4.19).

St. Paul, the greatest of the Apostles, carried the message of Christ to more people and more nations than any other Apostle, and it was evident that throughout his magnificent crusade no one was closer to him than Aquila and Priscilla. The fact that this couple had such a close relationship with St. Paul is itself enough to insure their immortality. Yet they were much more than favorites of Christ's chief vicar. Their mutual affection stemmed from their common purpose of bringing the hope of Jesus Christ to all peoples, a glorious effort in which all three were to share joys and sorrows.

At a dangerous time for Christians when Roman agents were lurking in every corner and were bent on throwing Christians to the lions, Aquila and Priscilla labored for Christ without regard for their own safety. They were not fed to the lions, but the Church Fathers tell us that they were put to death for their steadfast belief in Jesus Christ. They were beheaded, as was their beloved St. Paul, because the law specified death by the sword for Roman citizens.

This gentle pair was a source of great joy to St. Paul, the supreme Apostle of Christ, and for that alone they merited a place in heaven. Moreover, they were an inspiration to countless Christians. It is because of the selfless devotion of men and women like Aquila and Priscilla that we enjoy the strong faith of Christianity today.

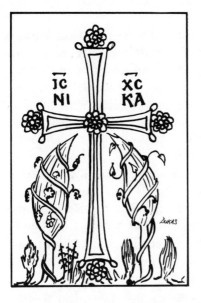

February 17

St. Auxibios of Soli, Cyprus

The island of Cyprus is unique among the islands of the world in that it has seen more history than some continents, and has come under the rule of conqueror, invader, and opportunistic warrior without losing its identity. Lost in this maze of Cypriot history is the little known fact that Cyprus also served as one of the cradles of Christianity. Nevertheless, its primary religious leader, St. Auxibios of Soli, came from another land.

Auxibios was as unique in ecclesiastical history as was the island of Cyprus. He was born of noble parents in ancient Rome. As a son of prominent aristocrats, he seemed an unlikely candidate for sainthood. The first seventeen years of his life were spent in the social graces of the period and in the pursuit of the pleasures of affluence in an unquestioning pagan society. Once he had received the best education and training, the young Auxibios forsook the ways of his parents. He chose to seek out the Holy Land in order to learn about the Christian faith he had heard about and thereafter to find his raison d'etre.

The ship he boarded sailed to Cyprus, marking the beginning of one of the greatest labors for Christ in the first century. St. Mark, who was to spend considerable time on the island of Cyprus, was responsible for Auxibios' conversion to Christianity. It did not take long for St. Mark to realize the genius and sincerity of his convert, and in due course he placed him under his personal care, teaching him the wisdom of the Master. Years of service to Christ passed and Auxibios was rewarded by being appointed Bishop of Soli. Shortly afterwards, St. Mark left for Antioch with the full knowledge that the Christian community in Cyprus was in the capable hands of his protégé.

The people of Soli were for the most part pagans. On his arrival in that city, Auxibios made it his first order of business to seek out the high priest of the temple of Zeus. He gained the confidence of this pagan priest with no difficulty. With consummate tact he brought about the conversion of the pagan priest, thereby obtaining a partner to assist him in bringing the message of Jesus Christ to the entire populace.

In a whirlwind of spellbinding oratory, Auxibios converted all of Soli. Soon a magnificent Church was built where all could worship as Christ had ordained. Years passed and the entire island was dotted with beautiful churches. Christianity flourished as no other place so isolated. Bishop Auxibios died in A.D. 105 and was laid to rest in honored glory in a crypt beneath the first church he had built so many years before.

Very soon after he had been entombed, there issued from the crypt of St. Auxibios a spring whose water was discovered to have the power of miraculous healing. According to Church history, many lepers anointed themselves with the water of Auxibios' tomb and walked away cleansed. These miraculous cures continued for many years until suddenly the water ceased to flow from the crypt. The feast day of St. Auxibios is celebrated on Cyprus with great ceremony and solemn splendor each year on February 17.

February 26

St. Photini
(The Samaritan Woman)

The incredible saga of the Samaritan woman rivals any other in fact or fiction. The story of her life is also the story of her remarkable family which lived during the early development of Christianity. In its scope and grandeur, her story reads like a passage from Homer; in fact, no amazon or superwoman of classical Greek literature could match the skill, courage, and spirit of this religious heroine.

The New Testament gives the familiar account of the "woman at the well," who was exiled from her native Samaria and was thus known as the Samaritan woman. According to the book of John (4:5-42), her life to that point had been anything but exemplary. However, she responded to Christ's stern admonition with genuine repentance, was forgiven her sinful ways, and became a convert to the Christian faith. Tradition has it that the Apostles of Christ baptized her and gave her the name of Photini which literally means " the enlightened one."

Without further ado, she set about bringing the word of Christ to others. She journeyed as far as Carthage on the African continent with the message of salvation, but not until she brought her sizeable family into active participation in the Christian cause. Photini had five daughters: Anatoli, Photo, Photes, Paraskevi, and Kyriaki. She also bore two sons: Victor (later given the name Photinos) and Joseph.

Following the deaths of SS. Peter and Paul at the hands of the tyrant Nero, Photini and her family traveled extensively, converting countless pagans to Christianity through her zealous faith in Christ. During the difficult days of Nero's persecution of the Christians, Photini and her family contributed to Christianity beyond measure. Her son Victor became an officer in the Roman army even though he was a Christian. At first he managed to not incur the displeasure of his superiors because of his faith. Soon enough, however, his duties as an officer came into direct conflict with his Christian principles. He was put in charge of a detail whose mission it was to seek out Roman citizens who dared to acknowledge Christ. Refusing to obey such an order, Victor was brought to swift military justice not only for insubordination and treason, but also for his own admission of belief in Christ. His subsequent imprisonment and torture were brutally inflicted by his former comrades.

Hearing the tragic news of her son's punishment, Photini straightaway demanded and received an audience with Emperor Nero himself. In an impassioned plea for her son's life, she boldly spoke for the cause of Christianity. She told the disbelieving tyrant how the gentle Jesus is worshipped by the world as the Messiah and the Son of God. The astounded Nero could not but admire her quiet courage, but his seething hatred for Christians could not be subdued and he sentenced her and her family to prison. There they languished for two years enduring endless suffering. When Photini and her family of five daughters and two sons were at last put to death, it was the end of an unsurpassed labor for Christ and the beginning of immortality for the Samaritan woman who came to the well for water and was transformed into a wellspring of Christian faith.

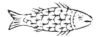

Δ. Δукаς

St. Paul the Simple

The best known saint bearing the name of Paul was, of course, St. Paul the Apostle of Christ, credited with having written more than half of the New Testament. In the fourth century, however, another Paul came forth. This Paul was to become a saint in his own right. Although he had no part in the writings of the Bible, he patterned his life after its teachings. The man was Paul the Simple, so called because of the simplicity of his life, not his intellect, and certainly not his dedication to Christ.

Paul the Simple was a farmer whose first full fifty years of life were lived in complete obscurity with no indication that he would ultimately attain prominence in Christian thought and deed. His sincerity in Christian endeavor was that of the average devout believer in Jesus Christ. He followed a quiet pattern of Church attendance and prayer. Outwardly he was a pious but unobstrusive, somewhat inconspicuous tiller of the soil who would scarcely have been expected to actively promote Christianity.

What stood in the way of his complete devotion to Christianity was his marriage to a girl several years his junior, whose ultimate infidelity left him a sadder but wiser man. Having done his best to preserve the marriage, and rewarded for his patience by his wife's leaving for other companionship, Paul the Simple found a noble purpose for his life. With high expectations he left for the desert and his true destiny.

His travels brought him into Egypt. There he sought out the greatest monastic figure of the day, St. Anthony, who was unimpressed by the farmer and suggested that he seek out some other approach to the throne of heaven. Now sixty years of age; Paul the Simple saw no reason to move. Therefore, for three days and nights he camped outside the cave of St. Anthony. The latter was thereby convinced of Paul's complete sincerity and welcomed him into monasticism. Thus at the age of sixty, at a time when most men look to a life of ease in retirement from life's daily struggles, Paul set about laying the foundation of his work for Christ that brought him due recognition.

He settled in a cave not far from that of St. Anthony. After a period of fasting, meditation, and prayer, he plunged into the work for God which he had so earnesty sought. Soon his tiny cave was a haven for those who sought the truth of Jesus and not long afterwards his reputation became as great as St. Anthony's, who then smiled whenever he remembered the way he had first slighted his strong friend Paul.

Paul the Simple acquired great intellectual power in his work for Christ and was said to have commanded a great power of exorcism. For this reason he was constantly consulted by troubled souls who found comfort in his gentle wisdom. His first fifty years of life were spent in obscurity; Paul the Simple's next forty years were those of comparative glory, for he lived to the ripe age of ninety. He died on 7 March 340.

March 14

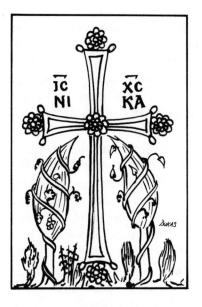

St. Benedict of Nursia, Italy

Although monastic retreats were never intended for any other purpose other than prayer and meditation, because of their strategic sites and formidable walls, they were often used by invaders for military purposes. The monastery atop Mount Cassino was no exception; during World War II the Germans transformed the monastery into a fortress. The citadel of peace was sacrificed to the bombs of the Allied Forces so that it unwittingly became a factor in shortening a terrible war and in bringing peace to all the world.

The monastery of Cassino was founded by St. Benedict and stood for centuries as one of the monuments to his Christian piety and dedication. That it was to be a battleground fifteen centuries later could not have been anticipated, but perhaps Benedict himself would have willed that the walls crumble under bombs so that peace might be restored. At any rate, the monastery has since been rebuilt and is as sacred now as it was before its demolition.

St. Benedict was born in the city of Nursia (Umbria) in A.D. 480 of the noble family known as Anicii— a great family that was to Nursia what the Medici were to be in Florence. The influence of affluent merchants, who were very cultured, brought to young Benedict every known advantage, including an education in Rome. However, the decadence of Rome and its society disenchanted Benedict. For this reason he turned his back on all that his family stood for and took to the hills in search of a meaningful life.

Abiding in caves and grottoes, Benedict allowed himself the luxury of one friend, upon whom he depended for his sustenance. Otherwise he chose to seek the real truth, beauty, and closeness to God found in the complete seclusion which allowed concentration without distraction. Over a span of three years as an eremite, Benedict discovered an approach to the service of God by isolation of not one, but groups of men. From this concept grew the monasteries that evolved into the order bearing his name.

Here was no martyr, no heroic gesture, no romantic journeying to foreign lands to propagate the faith. The quiet, humble ways of the monks of Benedict did God's work in obscurity, often with little recognition of their efforts toward peace on earth. It is said that they also serve who only stand and wait, but Benedict and his monks did more than stand and wait.

Young people from all walks of life were entrusted to the care of the monks, who saw to their spiritual needs together with their education. The ranks of the monks were swollen by those who had come to learn and had chosen to stay.

St. Benedict developed the rules of Western monasticism with such administrative and procedural perception that to this day there has been little or no change in the daily application of his concepts. With his two closest disciples, Maura and Placid, St. Benedict founded the renowned Monastery of St. Benedict on Mt. Cassino. This institution worked with the Church to the glory of God. His mission fulfilled, St. Benedict's life came to a peaceful end on 14 March 547.

March 15

St. Aristobulos

The outermost region of the world at the time of Jesus was the British Isles; they were as remote to the early Christians of the eastern Mediterranean as the reaches of outer space are to us today. The moat of the English Channel kept many travelers, friends and foes alike, from setting foot on this isle, but it was no barrier to the Apostle who dared to go that far from the land of the Savior.

After the Crucifixion and Resurrection of Jesus, a group of seventy men banded together who pledged to carry the message of salvation throughout the world. They were called the "Evdomekonta," from the Greek word meaning seventy. The man who undertook the trek to the western edge of the then-known world was Aristobulos, as hardy and dedicated a Christian as ever took up the cause of Christ.

Aristobulos was a favorite of St. Paul. What pleased St. Paul most was his tremendous missionary spirit and his willingness to journey to any area, friendly or hostile, just as long as he could take with him the word of God and the message of the Messiah. His unbridled enthusiasm made him the most likely candidate for the very difficult trek to the islands. In Romans 16:10, St. Paul's considerable respect for his friend is evidenced as he says: "Salute them which are of Aristobulos' household."

Wherever Aristobulos went in that uncharted land his encounters would have made lesser men retreat to more hospitable atmospheres. Nevertheless, with infinite patience and inspired persuasion his movement drew support.

With boundless energy and a cool detachment and disregard

for adversity, Aristobulos' labors bore fruit; the Christian Church in this forsaken land became a reality. His mission, which many viewed as the least likely to succeed, was fulfilled beyond expectation with the steady growth of Christianity and the establishment of churches. The British Isles became an integral part of the Christian world. The light of salvation glowed through the forest of the land that was to become a mighty empire, with no little thanks to its Christian character.

Aristobulos seems to have been spared persecution principally because the scattered array of opponents to his holy mission were put to rout by his oratory. Surviving many crises and dangers, he preached for many years until his voice was stilled by death on March 15. His feast day is also observed together with the other members of the "Seventy" on October 31.

March 22nd

St. Euthymios

The rugged mountains of central Greece, the Peloponnesos area, has produced illustrious sons who have added lustre to the history of Greece already crowded with heroic figures of both Church and State. Distinguished in this great company was Eleutherios, born and baptized in the village of Demetsana in 1796. He later came to be known as Euthymios of Constantinople. The son of a business merchant with holdings in Moldavia, he was to settle in Constantinople, the city with which he was identified. In his brief life span of twenty years Euthymios was to plunge into the depths of degradation, then scale the heights of glory in and emotional kaleidoscope.

While still a young teenager, Eleutherios journeyed to Constantinople. Along the way he visited Mt. Athos. This stop-over was to influence him later, when he sorely needed a spiritual revival. Having been educated in the finest schools, he was captivated by the civic charm of the grand old capital, and was very much at home there until hostilities broke out between Russia and Turkey. He made his way to Bucharest where a friend at the French Embassy welcomed him. In a few short months his life was to change.

Eleutherios fell in with a group of young Turks under whose influence he replaced his spiritual inheritance with that of the sensual hedonism of tribal sheiks. Gradually he gave way to a life of debauchery, spending his time drinking, carousing and in general, wallowing in sins of the flesh. He finally reached the point where, in a drunken stupor, he disavowed Christ, and to the howling delight of his disreputable companions, embraced their Muslim faith.

Not long after this shoddy display, Eleutherios was consumed by the spectre of damnation. With absolute repentance he fell to his knees asking for the forgiveness of Christ. It was then that Mt. Athos came into his mind's eye, for as he wept in contrition, he remembered his short but sweet visit.

In the holy confines of Mt. Athos, the youthful Eleutherios was reborn. He sought God in prayerful meditation and asked forgiveness for his foolish departure from the path of righteousness. He spent several months at the monastery of the Great Lavra in total dedication to the word of the Lord. A former Patriarch of Constantinople, Gregory, who had chosen to spend his declining years at the monastery, greatly aided Eleutherios in his acceptance of the monastic life. At the skete of St. Anne he was tonsured, being given the name of Euthymios.

He remained on the Holy Mountain long enough to become an instrument of God; many miracles were wrought by his hands. Euthymios felt compelled to return to Constantinople to support the besieged Christian faith. Once there, he was betrayed to the Turks and imprisoned for having mocked the Moslem faith in Bucharest and for his complete return to Christianity. On 22 March 1814, at the age of twenty, this Christian stalwart was beheaded. A tiny chapel on Mt. Athos is dedicated to his memory and every year special liturgical services are chanted by his brother monks.

SAINT
J
O
H
N
OF THE
L
A
D
D
E
R

D. DUKAS

St. John of the Ladder (Climacos)

The symbolic ascent to heaven is customarily portrayed by the flight skyward with angelic wings; one of our saints, however, depicts the ascension by the more practical use of a ladder. This symbolic ladder is to be scaled in a series of spiritual rungs where increasingly more exertion is required in order to see the Kingdom of God. The author of this approach was St. John of the Ladder who was one of the greatest writers in Christianity. "The Ladder of Perfection" is a treatise on spiritual exercises and actions which present in a brilliant and scholarly fashion and approach to the throne of Heaven.

Born in the sixth century, John spent the first sixteen years of his life in Palestine, the ancient Holy Land of his birth whose traditions he respected and whose Christian heritage he cherished. His early ambitions were realized when he went to the monastery of St. Catherine at Mt. Sinai, the oldest Christian monastery in the world. There he became one of the most scholarly monks in Christendom. The site of St. Catherine's was conducive to prayer and meditation, for there the scene of the burning bush took place and there Moses received the word from God himself. Moreover, to this place the grieving St. Helen, mother of St. Constantine the Great, came on a pilgrimage to the Holy Land some three hundred years before.

Mt. Sinai is unique in that it has been for centuries a holy magnet for Jewish, Moslem, and Christian pilgrims. While not as large or as imposing as Mt. Athos, Mt. Sinai still boasts of its antiquity and its prominence in the Old Testament. For that reason, John felt at home in this desert retreat and was inspired by this proximity to God to advance the cause of

Christianity in writings that have illumined the Church with their brilliance and clarity of thought.

John is remembered not only as the author of the masterful "Ladder of Perfection", but also as the originator of hesychasm, the divine quietness that leads one to God through constant prayer, the prayer which has come to be known as the pure or intellectual "Jesus Prayer." Regarding this John wrote: "Let the remembrance of Jesus be present with each breath, and then you will know that value of hesychia." He continued to champion this doctrine which found eager support among Christian thinkers, chief among whom was St. Gregory Palamas, whose sponsorship brought about official Church recognition of hesychasm in the fourteenth century.

For more than seventy years, John of the Ladder practised what he preached in the confines of his desert monastery. He achieved such a reputation for piety and wisdom that men from all walks of life were drawn to his side and came from all over the east to make a pilgrimage to his retreat. From John's strong faith and fervent prayer came the power of healing through the divine intervention of the Jesus. If nothing else, St. John's visitors would leave him with a serenity which they had never before experienced and with a sense of fulfillment that would last a lifetime.

At a time when Christianity was being tested to the fullest, St. John of the Ladder conveyed the divine grace that can only be achieved through Jesus Christ. He was able to advance the cause of Christianity without traversing the land, because the shining light which he received through his isolation with the Lord was carried out into the spiritual darkness by the grateful pilgrims who received his blessing. He witnessed no burning bush but he walked with God nonetheless. One of Christendom's finest figures, he died on March 30 at the age of eighty-six. His feast day is celebrated on the fourth Sunday of Lent.

March 31

D. Δukaʃ

Akakios,
Bishop of Melitene, Armenia

Unnamed and unnumbered Christians of the third century met death by violent and inhuman means as perhaps in no other century. Unique enough to become a saint of the Church was the courageous bishop of the early Church, Akakios, Bishop of Melitene, Armenia. Of those who laid down their lives by being tortured for the sake of Jesus, Akakios was tortured but somehow not killed. This departure from the classic stories of the saints has posed a never-to-be-solved enigma.

Nothing is known of Akakios' life prior to his emergence as an eminent religious leader of his time. A man of God, a scholar, a philosopher, and a dauntless standard-bearer of Christianity, Akakios was elevated to the post of Bishop of Melitene in Armenia. Church historians have credited Armenia with being the first country to establish Christianity as its national religion. In some measure this was due to leaders such as Akakios—leaders which Armenia provided and can point to with understandable pride.

Inevitably Akakios, who enjoyed wide acclaim as a spiritual leader among the Christian community, became bothersome to the pagan authorities. Emperor Decius was unalterably opposed to Christianity and condoned the atrocities committed against hapless Christians by his subordinates. By his order Akakios was arrested and put under the custody of Marcianus, the provincial governor of Cappadocia, for offenses against the state. This merely meant that Akakios was too good a Christian. When the dungeon door clanged shut behind him, Akakios knew what lay in store for him. However, he could never have anticipated the end result.

The governor was in no hurry to pass judgment, thus leaving him to the cruel devices of his jailers. Over a period of six agonizing months, Akakios was physically tortured to the point of near expiration, allowed to heal, and thereafter tortured again and again and allowed to heal. This vicious cycle of cat and mouse hardly left an area of his body without a scar. During the healing periods, however, Akakios wrote an impassioned and eloquent account of his faith in Jesus Christ. The script was a marvel of Christian devotion and was ultimately read by the Emperor himself.

Called at long last before the governor, Akakios expected to hear the death sentence. To his great surprise and to the astonishment of all who heard, the governor declared that by the order of Emperor Decius he was free to return to his Episcopal see at Melitene. This paradox has never been fully explained, although speculation has provided many versions. All accounts have some sound basis, but none has been proved. If nothing else, this turn of events served to mark Akakios as a unique saint in our ecclesiastical history. On March 31, late in the third century, Akakios died of natural causes, still bearing the scars to remind the faithful that he lived and died for Christ.

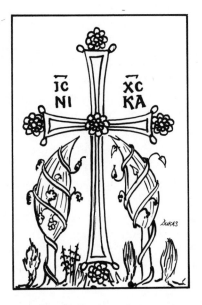

April 1

St. Mary of Egypt

A woman whose breathtaking beauty made her the center of all eyes experienced divine manifestation in time to find not only salvation in the Lord, but also eternity as a saint of the Church as well. Except for this chance encounter with the power of God, Mary of Egypt might have been just another pretty face in the society of man and a nonentity in the spiritual kingdom. Instead she came to reveal a purity of soul that overshadowed her physical beauty, and by way of a simple act of repentance, the gates of Heaven were opened to her.

Born and raised in Egypt during the reign of Emperor Justinian (527-565), Mary was unaware that her great beauty was the curtain which screened her from knowledge of the Christian lifestyle. In great demand among pleasure-seeking pagans, she knew only the clamor of the banquet hall. Pampered by those who sought her company, flattered by men whose wine flowed too freely, she lived in a narrow world of meaningless phrases and empty praises. She seemed destined to walk in eternal spiritual darkness, but that fate was never to be sealed.

It was not clear what brought Mary to the Holy Land. Nevertheless, she found herself in Jerusalem with her unusual entourage of suitors on September 14, when Christians were observing the feast day of the Elevation of the Cross of Christ. Not one to avoid any kind of celebration, Mary joined a group of Christians whose solemnity she thought strange. Nevertheless, out of curiosity she joined the line of march into the Church of the Holy Sepulchre, erected on the site of Christ's tomb. She experienced a peculiar delight in the silence of the procession which was a departure from the orgies to which she was accustomed. Mary was enjoying herself, but at that moment her life was completely transformed.

At the threshold of the Church entrance, Mary found herself powerless to enter, held back by some unseen power. For the first time in her life, she was stricken with the fear of something supernatural. As she turned to look upon her former companions, she now saw them as wretched and fled down the street in confusion. Pausing at last to regain her composure, she suddenly recalled another Mary of whom she had heard, the one the Christians called the Virgin Mary. At that moment she realized that her follies had prevented her entrance into the Church. In a fervent act of penance, Mary vowed to atone for her sins and to seek the way of Jesus, the Son of God.

This about-face is not new to those who have made the sudden discovery of the Lord, but Mary's case was unique not only for the way in which it was brought about, but also for the revelation of the beautiful soul exquisite enough to surpass her great physical beauty. From that moment on, Mary devoted herself to delighting in the work of the Lord where before she had delighted in the vain pleasures of the flesh.

With her new-found faith in Jesus, she turned her back on the sensual world to enter a convent in the desert. There she served as a nun in a sanctuary located on the banks of the River Jordan. To her lovely face was added the new dimension of the Holy Spirit and even in her stern garb she was a vision upon whom all looked with pleasure. Her noble spirit, however, was to emerge as her real beauty; and for forty years her spirit was one of the most compelling forces in the sixth century Christendom. With the zeal of the martyrs, Mary was a source of comfort and inspiration to the many who sought her, for they found the serenity of the divine in her exemplary service.

With the memory of the unseen barriers to the Church entrance ever-present in her mind, she lived in gratitude for her deliverance. Mary of Egypt has become known as the Penitent Saint, one whose name is synonymous with the Sacrament of Holy Penance.

SAINT JOSEPH THE HYMNOGRAPHER

ΔΔυκΔS

April 3

Joseph the Hymnographer

A writer of sacred music would hardly have been expected to lead anything approaching an adventuresome, perhaps stormy life. Yet that was precisely the kind of life led by one of the foremost writers of religious music. On the contrary, his life encompassed the controversial, the daring, and the adventuresome to the extent of rivaling Odysseos.

Joseph was born in the history-laden ninth century during the reign of the iconoclast, Theophilos (832). His early years in Sicily were uneventful even for such a quarrelsome period but his bravery asserted itself when the island was overrun by hordes of vandals and barbarians from the mainland. Because he dared to resist the invader, he was singled out as a prized trophy, sought by the vandals. After harrassing the enemy, and with the odds overwhelmingly against him, he managed to escape after several close calls. Joseph eluded the havoc wreaked by the invader by spiriting his family and himself out of Sicily to Greece, much to the consternation of the vandals.

This early chapter set the pattern for the rest of his turbulent life. Having settled in Salonika it appeared he would have had a trouble-free career when he joined the monastery of St. Antipas in Constantinople. But the serenity he sought was shattered when he took up the cause of the iconophiles during the iconoclast controversy. Emperor Theophilos had removed the icons from the churches and was severely punishing the iconophiles which dared to defy him. Not one to dodge an issue, Joseph joined the controversy vigorously, publicly defending the holy icons and openly defying the Emperor. Consequently, Joseph was persecuted, abused, and set upon with such intensity that he might as well have remained an elusive guerilla in Sicily. The great iconoclastic controversy reached its peak during this time. When several clergymen, Joseph among them, were banished for their opposition, he fled to Rome. After the death of Theophilos and the restoration of the icons, Joseph joyfully boarded a ship with the hope of enjoying a soothing monasticism. The ship never made port. Joseph was captured by pirates who cast him into a wretched prison in Crete.

In this implausible setting, Joseph started writing his beautiful hymns. During his years of imprisonment at the hands of pirates he prolifically composed the sacred music still sung in the Church today. He did not limit himself to his music writing, but also devoted himself to converting many of those about him to Christianity. His adventures continued.

After release from prison, Joseph acquired some relics of St. Batholomew and erected a church to the saint's memory. Later he was exiled when he criticized Emperor Bardas' divorce of his wife. After an exile of many years, he returned to Constantinople after the death of Bardas.

At long last Joseph was accorded the honor of a high position by the brilliant Patriarch Photios, who afforded him the opportunity to write his lovely hymns. This ultimately led to his recognition as St. Joseph the Hymnographer. The hymn writer who had eluded death many times, who had survived long imprisonment and long periods of exile and who had seen enough intrigue and excitement for a dozen lifetimes, died quietly in Constantinople on 3 April 886.

April 9

St. Eupsychios

The literal translation of the name Eupsychios is "good soul." A mother might hesitate to give such a name to her child fearing that it would prove too much to live up to. Yet, the name was given to the man we know as St. Eupsychios; he more than lived up to his name. He was born in the fourth century, the hundred year period which produced more saints in our Church than any other century since during this time Christianity was assailed by its gravest challenges. During these critical times, Eupsychios played an important part in the preservation of Christendom. In A.D. 313 Emperor Constatine declared Christianity an acceptable religion of the realm. However, even the conversion of the mighty Emperor was not enough to stamp out the paganism that stubbornly clung to every corner of the Empire. Some converted to Christianity only to revert to their former false worship; this grievously weakened the Christian religion. Among those who disavowed Christ was Constantine's nephew Julian.

Upon his uncle's death Julian succeeded to the throne. One of his first official acts was the restoration of the ancient hellenic paganism, the infamous act for which Julian, baptized a Christian, was branded as 'Julian the Apostate.' This wretched act did not constitute any outright denunciation of Christianity, nor did the shrewd Julian alienate the populace further with any persecution of the Christians.

Nevertheless the damage was done, and Christianity was placed in jeopardy in one fell swoop. An effective means of counteracting this menace had to take shape in a forceful and convincing manner. Julian, crowned a Christian Emperor, raised a powerful voice in support of the ancient hellenic gods. Thus, there was a great need for stronger voices in defense of Christianity.

Eupsychios was equal to the task despite the fact that he was of no holy order, nor was he a priest or bishop who could sound the alarm from a pulpit with authority. Perhaps it was even because he was a layman that he was to become more effective than the priest who chanted and prayed. He was a humble church-goer with an equally devout wife; together they symbolized the ordinary worshippers of the mighty Christian Church. When he stepped out of these ranks to boldly carry the banner of Christ in an answer to Julian, he became a force to be reckoned with. He had no difficulty in summoning fellow Christians in a show of force that would hearten all who saw or heard him.

Setting the pattern for what we now know as demonstrations, Eupsychios assembled a throng of Christians at the site of the erection of a new pagan temple. Exhorting his friends to show the Lord's loathing for pagan temples, he led them in an assault upon the semi-completed edifice. In a short time it was reduced to rubble. His bold action encouraged the more timid Christians who, emboldened, became active participants in the Christian cause.

Julian's reaction was swift and sure, as was to be expected. Not daring to risk a general uprising by any retribution that would have taken lives, he banished those who participated in the destruction of the temple. The insidious Emperor had his revenge, however, and ordered the execution of Eupsychios. Julian was to meet his death shortly afterwards at the hands of the Persians, but not until he had seen the good Eupsychios beheaded. One of the greatest of the lay saints of the Church, St. Eupsychios met a martyr's end on 9 April 360.

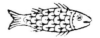

April 17

Agapetus I,
Pope of Rome

The separation of the Eastern and Western branches of Christendom came about through a slow unraveling of the Church fabric over many centuries. It was mainly due to the lack of sustained leadership needed to consistently bridge the ever-widening gap of philosophy between Rome and its sister cities of the Roman Empire. Since the Church structure was not unlike its state counterpart, the "all roads lead to Rome" concept led to recognition of the Bishop of Rome as the authoritative influence. The first Christian Emperor, Constantine, and his successors never gave official recognition to the Roman bishop's primacy of authority over the whole Church; popes were rarely accorded preeminence in Church affairs.

At the Council of Sardica (343) the Western bishops, with whom the Eastern prelates had already broken relations, recognized the supreme authority of the Bishop of Rome. After relations had been re-established, the Eastern sector was reluctant to submit to Roman authority in matters of discipline. Had every pope measured up to the standards of Pope Agapetus I, there would still be one unified Church of Christ. Too few had the qualities to be the catalyst that would keep the Church intact.

Although the papacy of Agapetus was to extend only two years, A.D. 535-536, his influence was to be felt for many years thereafter. The several years he served Christ prior to his ascent to the papal throne set an example which few have had the greatness to follow.

Agapetus had confined his service to Christ to Rome and its environs, exhibiting through the years a piety, wisdom, and spiritual strength that was to take him to the heights of Christianity. Upon assuming the papal throne, however, he decided that as the spiritual leader of all Christians in the Empire it was his duty to bestow his blessing upon the faithful in every part of Christendom. Thus, he traveled throughout Greece, heedful of the fact that until Victor I, the Bishop of Rome who seems to have been of African origin and knew only Latin, the single official language of the Roman Christian community had been Greek.

Church history relates that in his travels he was credited with performing several miracles of healing through the power of Jesus Christ. Moreover, he manifested his saintliness in many other ways. Welcomed to Constantinople by the Emperor Justinian, he plunged into the affairs of the Church. One of his initial acts was the prevention of Bishop Anthimos, a heretic and follower of Monophysitism, from becoming Patriarch. His personal selection, Bishop Menas, was to serve with distinction, proving himself at many times a credit to the Church.

Agapetus expressed a deep fondness for Constantinople. He would like to have remained there, but his duties called him elsewhere, and eventually to a triumphant return to Rome. He was a vicar of Christ in the greatest tradition of the Church, nobly serving Christendom until his death on 17 April 536, a date commemorated in special services each year in the Church of the Holy Apostles in Constantinople.

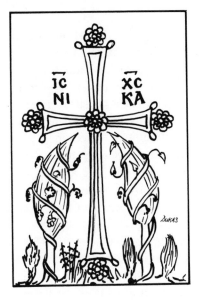

April 21

St. Alexandra

The sacrifices of the martyrs of the Church are myriad. There is no greater love than this last full measure of devotion. There are few, however, who prior to their last sacrifice had exchanged the splendor of a throne for the squalor of a dungeon for the sake of Jesus Christ. Yet such was the fate of Alexandra, wife of the Roman Emperor Diocletian (A.D. 282-304). The name Alexandra is synonymous with dignity and devotion because of the way the Empress bore herself in time of triumph and trial for the love of Jesus Christ and for all her fellow men of the Roman Empire.

Admired throughout the Empire for her consideration of others, a genuine concern that went far beyond the noblesse oblige customarily exhibited by royalty, Alexandra attained a popularity and prominence hitherto unsurpassed or matched since by an Empress. During one of her many benevolent tours of inspection for the state, her attention was drawn to the plight of a former Roman soldier who turned out to be St. George. It appeared that he was being excessively punished for refusing to worship the gods and for having declared himself a follower of Christ.

Alexandra decided to see for herself what was transpiring in the dungeons and arena in response to a compelling urge to see and talk to St. George. Her visit to the prisoner's cell became a revelation. The brutalized victim of Roman torture spoke to the Empress with calm assurance, dismissing his wounds as a small price to pay for the love of the Messiah. Before the evening was out, Alexandra had renounced the pagan gods and had joyfully accepted Christ as her Savior. Her fate was sealed, but nothing mattered except the love of Jesus and her concern for the man who had brought her to the Lord.

Alexandra wasted no time in going to her husband the Emperor to tell of her great discovery and to dissuade Diocletian from further torture of her new friend in Christ. The Emperor was annoyed at this and suggested that she had taken leave of her senses. When she persisted in pursuing her clemency plea for St. George, the Emperor's annoyance gave way to aggravation. When she doggedly insisted on mercy and tolerance in the name of the King of Kings, his aggravation became rage. At length, when he was convinced that Alexandra had been won over by the Christians, he ordered that she be cast into prison, thereafter to be beheaded along with St. George.

The three servants closest to Alexandra, Kordatos, Apollo, and Isaacion secretly arranged to see their mistress in her cell that night, only to find that she was willing to die for Christ. Furthermore, she declared that her husband would be cheated out of his revenge because she had a premonition that she would die before dawn. The distraught servants learned the following morning that Alexandra had died in her sleep. In a moment of tormenting grief they upbraided the Emperor for his cruelty, whereupon they too were put to death. Alexandra died on April 21. St. George was beheaded four days later on April 25.

April 27

Eulogios the Innkeeper

Swinging a sledge hammer in a stone quarry, his rippling muscles an indication of his prodigious strength, Eulogios gave the appearance of brute force in the manner of a sixth century Samson. Yet, Eulogios the Innkeeper matched every stroke of his powerful arms with a benevolent gesture of his generous heart. Hardly a candidate for sainthood by reason of his physical attributes or his high intellect, Eulogios nevertheless possessed those qualities of compassion and concern for the welfare for his fellow man that were ultimately to place him alongside those who have walked with God. Nevertheless, he was to show a weakness which nearly destroyed him in the eyes of God, but a weakness he was able to master.

In spite of the fact that he labored throughout the day in the bowels of the rugged earth, he was called the "Innkeeper" because by evening his house took on the appearance of an inn. Determined to share the fruits of his labor, he welcomed the poor and the dispossessed to his table. Over a period of many years he toiled solely for the purpose of being able to provide food for the hungry and shelter for the homeless as best he could afford. His self-denial and complete generosity marked him as a man of piety.

Laymen and monks respected him as though he were a man of the cloth. He formed lasting friendships with the poor and humble, the strongest bond being his attachment to the monk Daniel, whose admiration for the mighty stonecutter was boundless. Envisioning a center where the benevolence of Eulogios could be expanded to the greater benefit of mankind, the good monk prevailed upon a number of philanthropists and men of wealth to contribute to a cause which had been acknowledged as most worthy. In due course Eulogios was the recipient of considerable amounts of money.

The new-found wealth, spewing from all the sources the good monk could reach, was a temptation too great for Eulogios to bear. He convinced Daniel that there was a greater benefit to be meted out in the metropolitan areas, thus urging the monk to continue his soliciting. Eulogios moved from Egypt to Constantinople where, instead of establishing a refuge for the needy, he set himself up in a mansion with servants and embarked on a life of ease, if not excesses.

Eulogios totally abandoned the high purpose he had previously served. His religious training had been meager and his spiritual resistance to temptation was in no way enhanced by his physical strength. Consequently, he siphoned all the monies that Daniel had so diligently solicited and squandered them in lavish living. When Daniel discovered the sad turn of events, he hastened to Constantinople to implore his friend to return to his good senses, but to no avail. A dispirited Daniel returned to Egypt, praying for the salvation of his friend.

When news of Eulogios' misappropriation of funds reached the ears of Emperor Justinian, the injustice to the poor was brought to an immediate end, and stripped of his ill-gotten assets, a chastised Eulogios returned in disgrace to Egypt. It was not long before the kind Daniel sought out his misguided and woe-begotten friend, Eulogios the Innkeeper. Eulogios repented and together they prayed for the Lord to forgive the fallen stoneworker. Having gone from philanthropist to philanderer and back to philanthropist again, Eulogios took heart in the forgiveness of his sin, and with renewed dedication and vigor he once again became the stonecutter by day and the benefactor at his humble home by night.

When the infirmities of old age made his strenuous work in the quarry impossible, Eulogios retired to a life of prayer and meditation in the desert. Having conquered the evil of selfishness that had once seized him, his final years were devoted to God and he died a peaceful death on 26 April 585.

D. Δukas

May 5

St. Irene

A Christian in fourth-century Persia could scarcely hope to lead a peaceful life in the midst of various factions which leagued together in their common hatred and harassment of the followers of Jesus Christ. One woman who came to know the full wrath of the Messiah's enemies was Irene, whose name in Greek means peace. In choosing to follow Christ in this extremely hostile land of soothsayers and snake charmers, she chose to ride out the storm in a manner that brought her sainthood.

Born during the reign of Constantine the Great in the Persian city of Magydus, Irene was the daughter of Licinios, governor of the region. Licinios was a ruler of little humor, with even less understanding and with an iron will that was in the tradition of the Medes and the Saracens. He reared his only child, Irene, in an ornate palace. At the age of eight she began to be tutored in the grand manner of the times. Accordingly she studied for ten years under the tutelage of Apelanios, an educator renowned for his wisdom and intellect.

According to Apelanios, who was also Irene's biographer, an angel of the Lord appeared to Irene in a dream when she was a young woman and told her that she had been chosen to be the voice of the Messiah among her own people. When she told the venerable Apelanios of her dream, he stood in awe. When he saw it in its proper perspective he warned the girl that the road ahead would be strewn with obstacles and that the journey would be an arduous one. She knew that her faith would sustain her.

Licinios at first attributed her new eagerness for Christianity to the whim of youth, and he advised her to give up this madness. When her declarations for Christ continued unabated, he sternly warned her that he could tolerate no more. When she failed to comply he flew into a rage, threatening to have her trampled in the arena by wild horses. Apelanios related that while Licinios was at the arena arranging the stampede to take his daughter's life, he was somehow accidentally trampled himself.

Irene hurried to the side of her father, and as he lay mortally wounded she prayed to the Lord that he be spared. Her prayer was answered. Licinios recovered, repented, and was baptized into the Christian faith. For this he was promptly removed from office by the Persian King, Sedecian.

Turning to Irene, whom he considered a sorceress, Sedecian stated that he would restore her father to his post and allow her to go free if she disavowed Christ. She declined and was thereupon cast into prison. There she was subjected to inhuman torture and was given just enough food to sustain her until the next flogging. After Sedecian's death, she was released.

Miraculously regaining her health, she carried the message of the Messiah throughout the land, converting thousands to Christianity. Three consecutive successors to Sedecian, Savor, Noumerianos, and Savorian all failed to halt Irene's advancement of Christianity. Further imprisonment, torture and abuse of mind and body having failed, it was decided that Irene should be put to death. She was beheaded on 5 May 384.

SAINT

CHRISTOPHER

Δ.ΔUKAS
1976

St. Christopher

Many of our saints are pictured in icons and other representations as having great physical beauty. One of our better known saints was not so endowed. In fact, he was ugly and repulsive to those who first saw him and had no inkling of his great spiritual beauty. Yet, his ugliness does not seem to have been a hindrance to the mission he so nobly fulfilled in his lifetime.

Christopher's unwholesome appearance caused his comrades to call him "dogface" when he was a soldier in the Roman army. In some icons, Christopher is pictured as a saint with the head of a dog. Nevertheless, whereas physical beauty is skin deep, the beauty of a spirit such as Christopher's knows no bounds.

Although Christopher has been venerated as patron saint of travelers in the Western Church, the Roman Catholic Church, the Eastern Orthodox Church does not remember him in this way. This is primarily because no accounts in Eastern history associate him with travelers. However, at one point in his life, according to some sources, he demonstrated his Christian charity by carrying travelers across a river on his back. One day he chanced to carry a child across the river. At midstream the child's burden suddenly became staggering, and Christopher declared: "Had I borne the whole world on my back, I would not have outweighed you." Whereupon the child replied: "Marvel not for you have borne upon your back the world and Him who created it." For this reason Christopher is sometimes represented in religious pictures as fording a stream with the Christ Child on his back.

Christopher was born with the name of Reprobus, and

lived during the reign of the Roman Emperor Decius (A.D. 250). Although he served in the imperial Roman army, military life was not for him. An enthusiastic convert to Christianity, he was given to speaking out against the cruelties inflicted upon the followers of Christ. He could see no threat to the Empire by people whose primary purpose was the promotion of love and peace among all men and all nations.

In due time the soldiers of Decius were sent to arrest Christopher. The group had no difficulty recognizing the starkly hideous face of their former comrade-in-arms, nor had they forgotten the beauty of his gentle spirit. They were hesitant to carry out their order of arrest, but Christopher reassured them that he considered it a purely official matter. Personally, he said, he would prefer that they also receive the same light which shone upon him. He spoke to them of the Christian faith, the love of God and His love for all mankind.

The soldiers decided to accompany him to Antioch (Syria) rather than to drag him to the cruel justice of the Emperor. Reprobus was then baptized Christopher by Bishop Babylas, who also baptized the soldiers. Thereupon Christopher induced the soldiers to fulfill the order of arrest lest they come to know the emperor's wrath for disobedience. With sadness and reluctance they returned to Rome with their prisoner and brought him before the Emperor, who assumed that Christopher had been captured after an exhaustive search. Tried and convicted, Christopher was beheaded on 9 May 255.

May 10

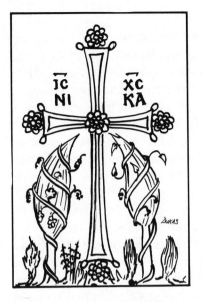

St. Simon the Canaanite

At the time of Christ there were factions which sprang up and oppressed the people at the mercy of the Roman tyrants. Various movements of religious and political natures often blended into a common voice against the oppressor. Among these groups seeking to recuperate the soul and spirit of man, as well as to remove the yoke of tyranny, was a group that came to be known as the Zealots. From this band emerged a man destined to become the eleventh Apostle of Christ—a man called Simon. Because of his energies within the movement, he was known as Simon the Zealot; sometimes he was referred to as Simon the Canaanite because he was born in Cana of Galilee.

It follows that such a man with enthusiasm for the cause of justice would be caught up in the whirlwind of Christ's message. Simon, therefore, became a mighty force in the salvation of his fellow man through acceptance of Jesus Christ as the Son of God. His inspired dissemination of the word of Christ had a profound influence on the early formation of the Christian religion; his contribution to its everlasting glory is immeasurable. His eloquent oratory poured forth in ceaseless effort to bring to every living person the truth and beauty of Jesus.

Simon was the bridegroom at whose wedding Jesus appeared. His wedding feast was the scene of the Lord's first miracle, the changing of water into wine. More important than the act itself—that of a true miracle—was the fact that it established the divinity of Christ and was an indication of the many wonders to come.

As a Zealot, a member of the semi-revolutionary party organized in A.D. 6 to 7 to resist the census ordered by the governor Quirinius, Simon was an anti-Roman reactionary who also became a pro-Jesus standard-bearer. According to Holy Tradition, Simon was present at the first Pentecost, where he pledged his life to spreading the message of Christianity where-ever he could make himself heard.

With other Apostles, he embarked on many missionary journeys to remote and often hostile corners of the then-known world. He carried his crusade for the acceptance of Christ into Africa and Mauretania, where he established the first of his many Christian churches. An innovator and visionary, his winning ways won converts where others failed.

Simon's ardor brought him to the deeply pagan land which is now England, where he was to spend his remaining years. The record of his word in England is clouded by a dark early history of paganism in this region, but it is known that he never ceased to preach the gospel, not even when he was finally set upon by the hostile heathens and tortured to death. The feast day of St. Simon is celebrated on May 10.

May 15

St. Pachomios the Great

Among the least known yet most venerated of our many saints was Pachomios, whose obscure life was such that his distance from man placed him closer to God, and yet he served both. Pachomios was one of the first monastics and the founder of communal monasticism.

Monasticism is not only one of the most sincere expressions of piety, but it is also one of the sturdiest pillars of the Christian faith. Monasticism is directed toward the attainment of the highest spiritual peace and serenity through prayer and meditation. The monastic thereby strives to attain likeness to God, in whose image all men are created. Those who look upon monastics as mere recluses seeking to avoid the harsh realities of life would do well to remember that without the strength of spirit and mind that the monasteries have provided, the light of Christianity would have been considerably dimmed, if not extinquished altogether.

Some of our greatest Christian stalwarts have been drawn from the monastic ranks. Their dedication to knowledge, wisdom, and faith in their eternal search for truth have been like those of the unheralded scientists whose microscopes have revealed the secrets that have helped mankind. The monk has often been the answer to both the apostate and the heretic.

The saint we honor for his endeavors in this much maligned but forceful and viable segment of Christianity is Pachomios. He was born during the reign of Constantine and was a soldier in the Byzantine army. Raised by pagan parents, he thoroughly enjoyed the military life with its pomp and splendor, but soon he discovered that he could perform greater service. He was not insensitive to his growing need for spiritual enlightenment and in an about-face he walked away from a life of conquest and riotous living, turning to one of earnest meditation and prayer. Bidding his parents farewell, he left the urban comforts of his native country, exchanging them for the barren wastes of the desert of Tavennisis in Egypt, to which he confidently strode for an unheralded approach to God.

His seeming estrangement from society developed into a greater intimacy with God, and after many years in retreat his reputation as a man of God was spread throughout the Empire. People were fascinated by the stories they eagerly would hear about Pachomios, the hermit, monk, intellectual, philosopher, and humble servant of God.

Within a decade, a total of twelve monasteries had been established in the desert by Pachomios. These monasteries were populated by those who followed him into the oppressive wasteland in search of God. The rules of monasticism laid down by him are still followed today. Such was his conception of the monastic approach to God that no one has ever sought to change it.

Many miracles came to be attributed to Pachomios; he attracted thousands who trekked mile after mile to be in his presence, to hear his counsel, and to receive his blessing. As a result, he was given the title of "great" by the Fathers of the Church. Unlike the martyrs, Pachomios came to a peaceful end in his beloved desert on 15 May 395.

Prince Boris (Michael) of Bulgaria

For several hundred years the boyars of Bulgaria had kept their country in spiritual darkness, in defiance of even their Tsar. However, they met more than their match in the ninth century in a ruler whose deliverance of Bulgaria earned him not only a place in history, but recognition by the Church as a saint. Combining an abiding piety with astute politics, Boris I brought Christ into the hearts of his Balkan countrymen, the Bulgars and Slavs. He eliminated the evil influence of the aristocratic boyars, whose fierce resistance to Christianity had impeded the cultural and spiritual development of what was to become a bastion of the Orthodox faith.

As son of Tsar Pressian, Boris was raised in an atmosphere not too far remote from that of the aristocracy which customarily scoffed at Christianity. In spite of this, he had become a most devout Christian when he succeeded to the throne in A.D. 852, a year which saw an important turn in the affairs of Bulgaria. His statesmanship in the unification of his scattered people was subordinate to the goal he set for the acceptance of Christ by all who dwelled under his rule. Seeking no outside help, he embraced the Christian faith as the state religion and set about its adoption throughout his land with the establishment of ecclesiastical authority, under whose jurisdiction they would come.

Both the papacy and Patriarchate of Constantinople, whose dogmatic conflict was widening the gap between them, sought to win Boris over. At length, Boris chose to come under the jurisdiction of Constantinople. Disavowing his allegiance with Louis the Frank, an arrangement which had precluded any treaty with the East, he met with the Byzantine Emperor Michael III in a historic moment for Orthodoxy and was baptized in 865, scarcely three years after he had come into power and set his Christian course. He even took the baptismal name of Michael, in honor of the Emperor, in a ceremony conducted by Patriarch Photios. Thus a new era for the Balkans was ushered in.

The true piety of Boris became evident when, to the surprise of those who knew him best, with his high hopes for his country fulfilled he decided to withdraw to a life of monasticism and named his son Vladimir to succeed him. His long-sought isolation was short lived, however, and he was forced to return to the state because of the ineptness of his son Vladimir as ruler. He found things in a sorry state and felt that he was doomed to serve as a Tsar. He decided that his great love of Christ would be better expressed by sacrificing the good of his country for his own spiritual attainment.

After some time, he again withdrew to monasticism. This time he placed in power his youngest son Simeon whom he had carefully groomed for the duties of his high office and had imbued with the Christian zeal that was to assure Bulgaria its place as a devoted ally of Constantinople. From the time Simeon replaced him in 893 until his death in 903, Boris was not known to have left the confines of his cloister. It is certain that he was kept informed of the civil and Church affairs, but he gave himself completely to the Lord for the last ten years of his life.

Other monarchs have abdicated the throne for various purposes, but none had abdicated for a higher purpose than Boris, who chose a life of austerity over a life of glamor. His desire to bring Christianity to Bulgaria not only had a profound influence over the Balkans, but his choice of Constantinople removed Bulgaria from the sphere of central Europe and caused repercussions within the framework of the Christian Church which later contributed to the schism which separated East and West.

The power struggle between Rome and Constantinople ultimately proved of advantage to Boris, who had longed for an autocephalous Church in Bulgaria, since it contributed to the early realization of this autonomy. Boris died, a true servant of Christ, with the knowledge that his country was, above all, a Christian nation.

May 20

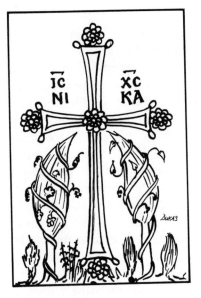

St. Thallelaios

Physicians of the third century did not have the benefits of modern science, hospitals and sophisticated life-sustaining machines, but they neverthe-less were surprisingly able to cope with many illnesses of mankind, to a degree of success that earned them the respect of prince and pauper alike. One who was able to cure the ills of his patients, not only with the medical skill he acquired in his profession but also with the miraculous help of Jesus Christ, was Thallelaios. His life story is unique among the saints because of the dual nature of his healing medically and miraculously through his dedica-tion to the word of the Lord.

Thallelaios was born in Lebanon during the reign of the Eastern Emperor Noumerias (A.D. 283-284). The son of Verou-kios, an archpriest of the Church of Lebanon, Thallelaios exhibited at an early age the scientific curiosity and skill that convinced his father he would make an excellent physician. To that end the boy's education was directed. While acquiring the medical knowledge and the best education possible, the youth never let his scientific interest crowd out his respect for God; he was as zealous a follower of Jesus Christ as he was a student of medicine. Seldom in Church history has there been a man of such combined passion for the exactness of science and the pure truth of the Lord.

Established as a physician, as well as a man of deep piety, Thallelaios converted his home into a clinic for all who sought relief at his hands. No one was turned away, and only those who could afford it paid a fee for his services. On Sunday, when he could have rested from his long labors, he went out instead to preach the word of Jesus Christ, always reminding them that "of the most high cometh healing." His impassioned oratory brought many into the fold, the healthy as well as the sick. Soon he was looked upon with awe because he performed miraculous cures which could only be effected through Jesus.

Since Lebanon was still ruled by pagans, it followed that when Thallelaios' work came to their attention, the physician became a hunted man. Nevertheless, he traveled throughout the country, carrying on the work of the Lord which he had accepted with great humility and dedication. In his travels he was exposed to the treachery of those who would see him cut down. In due course he was apprehended and brought before Theodore, governor of the province of Cilicia, whose fiendish delight was to wreak all manner of destruction on the Christian Church and its champions.

Priding himself with no small talent in debate, he hurled a challenge to Thallelaios to argue their opposing religions. Little did he know that he was taking on as an adversary not only a man of great oratorical power, but a man who had the might of the truth on his side. The debate soon turned into a defeat for the governor and his gods. Seeing the futility of his course, Theodore ordered the physician to be tortured. Through past experience the governor presumed that a punishment of the body would break the spirit and he would emerge victorious after all. Such was not the case, however, and after all forms of cruelty had failed to crush his spirit, Thallelaios was ordered to be executed.

It was the end of the third century, on May 20, that the glorious physician Thallelaios was beheaded. This martyr exemplified in his lifetime the highest order of mankind created in the image of God.

May 21

SS. Constantine and Helen

The tricentennial anniversary of Christianity, when dated from the actual birth date of Jesus, had passed by a dozen years before it came to be recognized as the true Faith by an emperor, the ruler of the civilized world comprised of the Roman Empire. It was in A.D. 312 that Constantine, who was to become known as the Great and who was the Emperor of Gaul, displayed to all the world his conversion to Christianity when his legions defeated the rebellious forces of Maxentius at Turin under the banner of the Cross. Also, while Emperor of York, he made his mother, Helen, the dowager empress in 306. This she remained throughout her lifetime, having a mother-son influence on Christianity that has never been duplicated.

Helen, reputed to have been a British princess and the daughter of the King Cole one hears of in song, gave birth to her illustrious son at Naissus in the lower valley of the Danube on February 17 of a year presumed to be in the mid 280's. Because of her lineage she is as much revered in Great Britain, as is evidenced by the many churches, principally of the medieval era, dedicated to her memory. She is also said to have discovered the Cross of Christ during a tour of Golgotha. In her declining years her pilgrimage was in part motivated by the mysterious death of her gransdon Crispus and brought about the erection of beautiful Christian Churches at the sites of the Nativity, the Holy Sepulchre and the Ascension, as well as at others. For this and her son's equally pious work, the mother and son have been recognized as equal to the Apostles and are so commemorated in a common feast day of the Church.

It has been said that Constantine the Great turned to Christianity for political convenience, but that hardly is the case. An emperor with his power and stature had little to gain from currying the favor of the Christians, which were at best of minor importance to the community and had become so weakened by the divisiveness in their own ranks that they were threatened with extinction. Constantine told of having seen a cross of light in the sky just prior to his successful campaign against Maxentius and from that moment forward embraced the Christian Faith, becoming a servant of God chosen to kindle the flame of Christianity to a brilliance it would not have otherwise known. From a weak and divided community, Christianity burst forth under the leadership of Constantine to become the official religion of the realm and swelled in numbers that assured its power and permanence.

The campaign against his enemies was brought to a successful conclusion by Constantine at the ancient City of Byzantium, which he decided to rebuild on a grand scale and to rename Constantinople, symbolizing its imperial flavor and Christian zeal. It was by design a Christian city, free of pagan temples and embellished by many magnificent cathedrals and churches to the glory of God and His Son Jesus. It was Constantine who made Sunday a public holiday and to him goes the credit for healing the wounds within the Church itself, which he declared to be an affront to God and for which he labored, together with the various bishops, to bring about compromises that would put all Christians on common ground.

The doctrine of Arianism that so divided the Christian family was met with firm action by Constantine, who called for an ecumenical council at Nicaea held on 20 May 325. It was attended by an imposing array of church dignitaries, all of whom, however, were overshadowed by the dominant figure of the great emperor, and whose great influence brought about the signing of the historic Creed. Although the unity with which the Council had formed was to meet with resistance in some corners, subsequent councils and meetings with Church greats are the legacy of Constantine, who so piously gave the Christian Faith the great strength that in later years enabled it to survive the onslaughts of such as Julian the Apostate.

Helen died in 328. Her son Constantine died on 21 May 337 A.D. The reign of Constantine has proved to be the greatest of any ruler in history, not only for Christianity but for the entire world as well.

May 22

St. John of Vladimir

Many more paupers than princes have attained sainthood. One reason for the scarcity of royalty's representation to the highest Church ranks lies in the fact that to serve as a head of state, while at the same time serving God to the fullest, calls for a man of exceptional caliber. One who had this rare quality was John of Vladimir, Bulgaria. His father Neeman and his grandfather King Simeon were of the royal house that ruled in Ochrid. John's mother Anna, also of royal blood, claimed direct kinship to the regal court of Basil of Byzantium.

Born near the end of the tenth century, John was reared in a royal household dedicated to Orthodoxy where respect for God took precedence over the affairs of State, no matter how solemn. His chief tutor was Bishop Nicholas of the Slavonic Diocese of Bulgaria, who remained close to John, officiating at his marriage to the daughter of King Samuel and crowning him when he ascended the throne after the death of his father. He came to power as King of all Serbia as a true monarch and a true Christian. He set an example for all his coutrymen to follow with his sincere desire to serve, but with emphasis on the common need to serve God. This he did with a dedication that was to have a tremendous impact on the Orthodox faith, not only in Serbia, but throughout the world.

Under his direction Serbia embarked on an expansion of Orthodox influence through the development of spiritual and cultural centers made possible by a broad program of newer and larger churches, monasteries, hospitals, schools and seminaries. John's Christian zeal bore much fruit. He delighted in mingling with his brethren at Church services and religious functions.

An excellent horseman, John of Vladimir enjoyed riding in the solitude which he felt brought him closer to God and nature. While riding one day, John saw an eagle flying against the sun. From its neck hung a golden cross. This sight was similar to Emperor Constantine's vision of the great sign of the cross in the heavens when he heard the words "EN TOUTO NIKA," or " in this sign conquer." John followed the flight of the bird, which alighted at the feet of an angel of the Lord. In a moment the angel and the eagle were gone, but on the spot laid the golden cross, which he took to his bosom. In prayerful gratitude he erected a beautiful Church and monastery on that site.

John interpreted this as a call to the service of God; thus his monarchy became secondary. Leaving his duties to be carried out by subordinates, he went to his holy spot in the forest for meditation and prayer. While the country flourished under his established methods, political intrigue in the royal court was spurred to action by the King's absence under the influence of the King's wife. She envied his devotion to the Church and saw an opportunity to establish herself as absolute ruler. She conspired with her brother to assassinate King John, and was provided the exact circumstances for success when both her husband and brother answered the call to battle against Basil of Byzantium.

In the campaign King John's brother-in-law waited until John was engaged in furious combat, then treacherously thrust his sword into the unsuspecting King. John lies buried at the Chapel of the Holy Cross. Because of the many miraculous cures at his grave site, John was later canonized a saint. His feast day is observed on May 22.

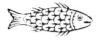

May 28

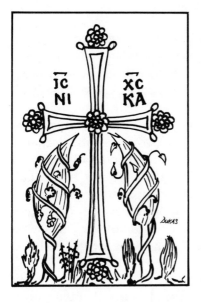

St. Zacharias of Prusa

By the turn of the nineteenth century the oppressive yoke of the Islamic Turks had been borne by Christians for four hundred years. With no deliverance in sight, Christianity continued to flourish despite concerted efforts on the part of the relentless enemy of Jesus Christ to destroy his truth. For the Turk, the greatest feat was the conversion of a Christian to Islam. To this end they bent themselves with maniacal cunning and cruelty. A man who was to meet their opposition and emerge more Christian than ever was Zacharias, a resident of Prusa.

Zacharias, the priest of the small parish of Kaiambasi, fell a victim in 1802 to alcoholism, which was as much a disease 170 years ago as it is today. Zacharias fell prey to this ironically through the necessity of priests to drink the remaining sacrificial wine of the Eucharist. He soon found himself drinking more and more until at last he had difficulty in remaining sober.

In a drinking bout with some of the Turks, who were constantly ready to take advantage of a weakened foe, Zacharias drank himself into a state of complete intoxication. While in a state of alcoholic stupor and swayed by his leering companions, he disavowed the Christian faith and mumbled an acceptance of the Muslim faith. In fiendish glee, the Turks dressed him in Arab garb, plied him with more and more wine, and led him in mock triumph through the streets — to the utter horror of the members of his parish.

The Turks could not keep Zacharias drunk forever, and they soon tired of their sport. When they left their unfortunate prey to his own devices, Zacharias soon realized his folly. He sought the comfort of his parish, but received no comfort from his parishioners. After considerable agony of both body and soul, he summoned enough strength to abstain from alcohol. In repentance he went about righting the wrong he had done, publicly declaring his mistake.

Having cleansed his soul in contrition in his parish church, and having once again donned his priestly garments, Zacharias received an audience with the Turkish magistrate. He appeared before the magistrate so that all might know his true belief, which he vowed never again to renounce no matter what the circumstances. This earned him not only the renewed respect from the Christian community, but also the wrath of the Turks, who then accused him of having made a mockery of their faith, a most grievous offense.

Zacharias found himself in the squared confines of a prison cell, facing the vengeance of a system of justice that only knew extreme cruelty. To no avail they heaped torture after torture upon the unfortunate prisoner, only to observe him praying to the Lord for his deliverance. With full knowledge that he had received the Lord's forgiveness for his sin and His blessing for his true faith, Zacharias met a violent death at he age of thirty-eight. He was beheaded on May 28, attaining a martyr's crown.

June 5

St. Dorotheos

For those who have allowed themselves to believe that the Church has an abundant crop of saints, or perhaps even an over-supply, it would be wise to consider that the number is relatively small compared to the countless thousands from whose ranks they have been drawn. So many have given themselves totally to the word of Jesus Christ that one can only wonder how many sweet souls have been known but to God, and not to those churchmen whose task has been not only to seek out, but also to select the most deserving — a task made difficult by the eligibility of so many dedicated men and women of Christianity.

There could have been little question regarding the sainthood of Dorotheos, Bishop of Tyre (in Phoenicia) during the fourth century. His qualifications were such that he stood out at a time when the Church was blessed with extremely gifted and dedicated Church leaders. At any time in history, in any endeavor, Dorotheos would have established a reputation for himself. The turbulent fourth century summoned the utmost in a remarkably talented group of bishops who persevered for Christ. Of these, Dorotheos emerged as a standard-bearer of unbridled enthusiasm and extraordinary literary talent. As a Biblical scholar, his writing clearly displayed his proximity to God.

The writings of Dorotheos comprise a small library of flawless literature spanning many aspects of the Christian religion including an interpretation of the Bible unmatched in clarity of thought and philosophic deduction. At the height of the Diocletian persecutions, which were followed by those of the equally relentless Licinius, Dorotheos was so absorbed by his interpretations of the Old and New Testaments that he scarcely noticed the approaching danger of arrest. He was virtually thrust out of the path of danger by close friends and he fled from Tyre for the safer locale of Dyssopolis in the European province of Thrace. Here he wrote articles on the Orthodox faith which are to this day admired for their clear thoughts and depth of insight.

A master of many languages, Dorotheos spent a number of years in Rome, where he had been commissioned to write a history of the Apostles in Latin. With the death of the Emperors Diocletian and Licinius, the prolific pen of Dorotheos produced literary and religious masterpieces that are milestones in the development of the Christian faith. He was approaching old age when the infamous enemy of Christ, Julian the Apostate, became Emperor. Julian denied the Christian faith into which he had been baptized, and then he embarked on a terrifying campaign against Christians that marks one of the darkest chapters in Christian history.

The aging Dorotheos—he is reputed to have been a centenarian—was caught up in this fiendish net of persecution. He was put to torture with no regard for the infirmity of his old age. The frail author, whose literary contribution was matched by his spiritual blessing in the Christian community, succumbed to the tortures of the pagans. Dorotheos, whose name means "gift of God," died on 5 June 363, leaving behind a legacy to endure as long as Christianity itself.

SAINT OF

C Y R I L

A L E X A N D R I A

Δ. Δукαs

June 9 (and January 18)

St. Cyril

Under the direction of Julian the Apostate, the altars of paganism burned anew, threatening Christianity in the early fifth century. The thrusts at the heart of Christianity by such a powerful adversary as the Emperor were warded off with the skill and courage of men such as Cyril of Alexandria, who met the challenge and hurled it back. Thus he not only preserved intact the Church of Christ, but added to its strength and expanded its sphere of influence. Cyril not only drove off the forces of evil that encircled Christendom, but he was also successful in bringing an end to the internal conflicts within the Church.

An Alexandrian Greek, Cyril was an Egyptian national leader as well as a theologian. Born in A.D. 375, he had a talent for combining politics with religion which was helpful to him, but would also cause some disagreement among his biographers as to his true character. He was, above all, an able and influential theologian while at the same time a shrewd politician. His involvement in politics brought down on him much criticism by those who opposed his views. However, this was not enough to prevent his being honored as a doctor of the Church.

Succeeding his uncle Theophilos to the see of Alexandria in 412, his episcopate was at odds with the prefect Orestes. When Cyril closed the churches of the Novations, a schismatic sect led by Hypatia, a friend of the prefect who had been killed in a riot which Cyril was unable to forestall, Orestes' hostility was intensified. To bring about peace, Cyril acknowledged the rights of civil authority but remained the leading citizen of Egypt. Turning to religious matters exclusively, he wrote commentaries on selected passages of the Pentateuch, Isaiah, the minor prophets, and on the Gospels of John and Luke.

The stage was set for conflict within the Church when Nestorios of Antioch became Patriarch of Constantinople in 428. In an affront to Orthodoxy, he refused to call the Virgin Mary "Theotokos" which literally means "God-bearer" or "Mother of God." Objecting to this departure from accepted Christian tradition, Cyril wrote a series of treatises which recognized the fullness of Christ's humanity by insisting that the term "Mother of God" signified the union of Christ's divine and human natures, made one at the Incarnation. This brought about an exchange of anathemas between Cyril and Nestorios that culminated in the convoking of a council to settle the dispute. This council, which was convened by Cyril, condemned Nestorios before the assembled bishops; Cyril in turn was condemned by John of Antioch, spokesman for Nestorios. Ultimately, the council, which had been convened in Ephesos in 431, supported Cyril and banished Nestorios. True peace for the Church was not restored until 433, when Cyril accepted a revised statement on the two natures.

In answer to the apostasy of the Emperor, Cyril wrote the brilliant literary work, "Against the Galileans," in which he exposed the fallacy of Julian's pronouncements. The prominence of Alexandria in Church affairs declined in the late years of Cyril's life; this leadership was transferred to the imperial city of Constantinople. During his lifetime, Cyril's achievements kept Alexandria in the forefront of religious activity and influence. Ranking among the greatest of the Church fathers, Cyril died in 444.

June 14

Δ. Δukas

St. Methodios,
Patriarch of Constantinople

Differences of opinion in a healthy climate where mutual consideration is maintained at all times can be beneficial to those who have opposing points of view; when carried to extremes these differences of opinion lead to crises or disaster. The iconoclastic movement, which sought to remove the holy icons from Christian churches and homes, caused a near disaster to Christianity. It threatened the structure of Christendom for more than 150 years. That this controversy did not completely ravage the framework of Christian worship is due to the stand taken by a few stalwarts, among whom was Methodios, Archbishop of Constantinople and a champion of the preservation of the sacred icons.

Methodios opposed the iconoclast view that the icons themselves were being venerated. He insisted that as symbolic representations they should be maintained as the founding Fathers of the Church had planned. An erosion of this basic concept would have unnerved the might of Christianity and stripped it of its authority, thus reducing it to a philosophic expression. Without Methodios and others defending tradition against the flood of controversial iconoclasm, the Christian Church would not be as we know it today.

Born in the city of Syracuse in the ninth century, Methodios followed the time-honored paths to religious greatness, preparing himself for the service of Christ through intensive study and zealous application to the glory of God. Well versed in philosophy, dedicated to the dissemination of the word of Jesus, and pious in all endeavors, he placed himself in a monastery in

Henolakkos, near the ancient city of Byzantium. With attention to every detail of prayer and worship, he soon became abbot of the monastery.

The next step in Methodios' glorious career was his appointment as Archbishop of the Diocese of Kyzikios. Here his reputation as a complete man of God was forged through his tireless efforts for the betterment of mankind and the spiritual elevation of those about him. His fame spread through the Empire. About this time Emperor Leo the Armenian, an avowed iconoclast, assumed power; his successor, Michael the Stammerer, continued Leo's iconoclastic policies. The resulting polarization paralyzed the Church. When Methodios boldly sought to stave off the forces of Michael, he was rewarded by exile to the tiny island of Antigone, near the Bosporus.

While an outcast, Methodios was subject to humiliation and hardship. Although there was no evidence of physical torture while on the island, nevertheless he was badgered and embarrassed. This mighty voice of the Church was systematically reduced to a whisper with the ultimate end being his complete silence. He was removed to Constantinople and further demeaned by being placed under guard. The iconoclast did not dare to inflict cruelties upon such a popular bishop for fear of arousing the populace.

Methodios was not to be silenced, however. Gradually his firm stand against the iconoclasts came into full view and he was once again able to speak out against those who would reduce the churches to barren timber and stone. His sentiments were echoed throughout the Empire when Emperor Theophilos died. His wife and successor, Theodora, offered him her official support.

In recognition of his contribution to the Church, Empress Theodora brought about the appointment of Methodios as Patriarch and together they convened an Ecumenical Council which declared on 11 March 843 that icons were reaffirmed as an integral part of Christian worship. He died on 14 June 858.

95

June 21

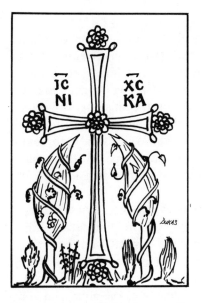

St. Julian of Egypt

Egypt is best remembered as a land of antiquity whose ancient civilization was responsible for the awesome pyramids and the inscrutable sphinx. Despite its association with the Middle East, Egypt lies on the African continent and not in Asia. During the reign of Diocletian in the third century, Egypt was a Christian wellspring. The land of the Pharaohs, which had sheltered the Virgin Mary, Joseph, and the Christ Child when they fled from Bethlehem, also offered shelter to countless Christians in the years that followed. In this era the most noted Christian benefactor was Julian of Egypt.

Julian of Egypt was responsible for the founding of a spiritual haven consisting of a cloister of monasteries that possibly housed as many as twelve thousand monks, laymen, and Christian refugees at one time. While not matching the colossal pyramids for sheer spectacle, this monastic retreat was nevertheless a marvel in Christian history. A refuge for devout Christians fleeing persecution from all corners of the Empire, the center was conceived and organized under Julian's direction. For Julian, the viability of the Christian religion was his only purpose in life, a purpose which he fulfilled with great dedication.

The spiritual refuge was located in Antiopolis, which was governed under Diocletian by Marcian. Although Marcian's political image was somewhat obscure, he seized the opportunity to make himself known by persecuting those seeking refuge from persecution. Lacking imagination, and with little or no regard for consequences, he planned for the total destruction of the monastic center in one fell swoop.

Having received permission from the Emperor to deal with

Julian in his own way, Marcian plotted to set fire to Julian's haven. Under cover of darkness, while the unsuspecting Christians lay asleep, Marcian deployed his soldiers at strategic points surrounding the cloister, and at a given signal the torches were simultaneously applied. In the ensuing fire which raged with horrible devastation throughout the compound, hundreds of men, women, and children were burned to death; many hundreds of others received severe burns, and the remaining hundreds who managed to escape the fire were captured and imprisoned.

Among the survivors was Julian, whose heart was seared, if not his body. Even at the sight of the holocaust, Julian remained steadfast in his faith in Jesus Christ. There were those in the state who held Julian in high esteem for his piety and indomitable spirit. Among his secret admirers was the young man Kelsios, the son of the tyrant Marcian. Deeply touched by the tragedy, Kelsios secretly visited Julian on a regular basis in his jail cell and in a very short time converted to Christianity. Marcian was convinced that this was a spell cast upon his son. When the words had no effect on the youth, it fell to the ruler's wife to talk her son out of the spell, and she spoke to her son with a mother's love and understanding. To her husband's surprise, she became a Christian convert herself.

At this point, Marcian's political ambition and warped pride gave way to madness. More concerned with his political image in Rome than his responsiblilities as husband and father, he ordered the execution of his own family, along with other Christians, chief among whom was Julian, who suffered a martyr's death on June 21.

June 27

St. Sampson the Glorious
Innkeeper and Physician

It comes as no surprise that scientific skill of a sixth century physician could be combined with the devout worship of a zealous Christian with the result that he became a venerated saint of the Church. Sampson, who came to be known as the "Glorious Innkeeper and Physician," was such a man. His title is curious only until something is known about this rare man whose life was crowded with glorious accomplishments in the name of the Lord and for the benefit of mankind.

Sampson, a native of Rome, was descended from royalty through his father's kinship with the lineage of Emperor Constantine. His birthright assured him a life of comfort and glamor, but instead he chose to pledge himself to the service of God and mankind. The demands of his tasks were never too much to bear and he took great delight in them. Following the customary liberal and fine arts education, he applied himself exclusively to the study of physical medicine and spiritual philosophy, for which he exhibited a remarkable skill and insight.

He acquired an enviable reputation as physician and man of faith when, with the passing on of his parents, he transformed the family estate into a clinic and hostel for the physically incapacitated and the spiritually distressed. Within a short time, the word of his healing power of body and mind attracted so many people seeking both his physical and spiritual healing, that he found it necessary to hire a staff to care for the ever-increasing numbers. All his benevolence was at his own personal expense. When he was satisfied that his refuge was adequately staffed, he endowed the hostel with the total wealth willed to him, content to live in poverty. He then set out for Constantinople, the city he had for so many years yearned to see.

Sampson's reputation preceded him to Constantinople, and although he had hoped to live in relative obscurity, devoting the remainder of his days to asceticism, he found as much need for his services in this Byzantine paradise as there had been in Rome. Lacking the facilities which had been at his disposal in Rome, he settled in modest quarters contributed by a kind admirer and without ceremony set about waging a one-man war against disease and despair.

Sampson's holy work did not go unknown to Patriarch Menas of Constantinople. When Emperor Justinian fell ill and failed to get relief from his physicians, the Patriarch Menas suggested that the suffering Emperor summon the physician Sampson. The weary Justinian nodded assent; Sampson was rushed to his bedside. The physician's skill was equal to the occasion and the grateful ruler rewarded his healer with the establishment of a medical center that far exceeded what he had left in Rome.

Emperor Justinian is remembered as the man responsible for the erection of the Cathedral of Haghia Sophia in Constantinople. Although Sampson's medical center was not as grand as the Cathedral, it was as noble in purpose. There, Sampson continued to serve God and man until his death, which came peacefully on 27 June 598.

June 29th

St. Paul

Whenever the storms of controversy within the Christian Church have cast a shadow on the Cross of Jesus Christ, the clouds have been rolled back by the spiritual brightness, undiminished by the centuries, of the magnificent St. Paul. Most Christians agree that were it not for St. Paul, the new faith of Jesus Christ would never have taken hold to become the mainstay of Western civilization. The total commitment of St. Paul to the Messiah, for whom he ultimately sacrificed his life, brought the message of Jesus to the nucleus of Christians over a period of thirty years and assured the permanency of the truth of the Savior. If it can be said that Christ planted the seeds, then it was St. Paul who nourished the garden of Christendom.

St. Paul was born in Tarsus, a flourishing crossroads city in Cilicia, Asia Minor. He received his religious training in Jerusalem under the renowed rabbinical tutor Gamaliel, from whom he absorbed the teaching of the Pharisees with intensity and sincerity. He deplored the acceptance of the Messiah as heresy to his religion and as an affront to the Law of the ancient covenant. Armed with articles of condemnation from his council, he set out for Damascus with an avowed purpose of wiping out this new belief in Jesus Christ. On the road to Damascus he met Jesus. This is perhaps the most dramatic turnabout in history, one that was destined to alter the course of the world. St. Paul embraced as the Messiah the man whom he had set out to destroy; thereafter he devoted himself with deep conviction to the truth of Christianity. The conversion alone of this profoundly religious man is in itself testimony to the reality of the Messiah's divinity.

Although not one of the twelve disciples of Christ, Paul linked himself with the Apostles and became the greatest Apostolic missionary of all time. A brilliant orator and writer, he was sensitive to the needs and moods of the various tribes of both Greek and Near Eastern backgrounds. Furthermore, he was intelligent enough to cope with the problems that beset the new faith at every turn. A man of small physical stature, he cast a giant shadow upon the missionary scene as he traveled the length and breadth of the ancient Eastern world. He had success following success in the vast areas of Asia, Greece, Cyprus, Macedonia, and eventually Rome, where his most noble purpose was to prove his undoing.

He had a fondness for Jerusalem, for whose poor he continually solicited funds. Moreover, he envisioned a union of the Jewish and Christian communities, a project which was to prove dangerous. He met James in Jerusalem and together they sought a means to bring this laudable plan into being. However, he encountered not love but outright hostility. In fact, he had to be saved from an angry mob by the Roman authorities, who placed him aboard a ship bound for Rome, where he arrived after a tossed voyage. St. Paul had always wanted to use the eternal city with its strategic position in the empire, from which the spread of Christianity could be projected. Although he preached in Rome for two years, his ambitions were never completely realized, except for the production of his masterful Pastoral Letters.

Despite his frail health he continued his work for Christ at an accelerated pace, but his enthusiastic love for the Savior also brought him the resentment of certain influential elements in Rome. When his enemies had done their worst, he was brought to trial and met a martyr's death about A.D. 67.

The true greatness of Paul is discerned in his writings, particularly his epistles. As author of almost half of the twenty-seven books of the New Testament, he has influenced Christianity as no other man with the exception of Jesus Himself. Even after nearly two thousand years, St. Paul's candor, freshness, clarity, and perceptiveness in his writings are as welcome as sunrise. Christianity remembers St. Paul on June 29th.

July 7

D. Dukas

St. Kyriaki

During the third century Christianity was put to its severest test and met the challenge of its enemies through the quiet courage of its believers. One of the many victims of the pagan Emperor Diocletian was a young woman named Kyriaki. The details of her short life are not abundantly clear, but enough is known to understand the remarkable events which led up to her martyrdom.

Kyriaki was the daughter of the devout Christian couple Dorotheos and Eusebia, whose active participation in Christian affairs influenced their daughter's decision to serve Christ. Her parents had been childless for many years, and it was in answer to their fervent prayers that a daughter was born to them. Out of gratitude to the Lord, the child was named Kyriaki, which literally means, the "day of the Lord," the day of the week on which the Lord rested from His labor when He created the world.

Kyriaki managed to receive a full education at a time when the degree of literacy was very low and when education for a girl was reserved for the very privileged. She joined her parents in their intensive work for the Christian Church. By the time of her maturity the family had achieved an enviable reputation for missionary zeal. They accomplished this in the face of extreme dangers. In this hotbed of paganism they were constantly on the alert for those who would betray them to their enemies, who were eager to thin the ranks of the Christians. Thousands of Christians masked their true faith, worshipped in hard-to-find places, and won new converts daily despite every form of oppression and harsh justice.

When Kyriaki was about to enter into the service of Christ

as a nun, her parents, who were wanted desperately by the pagan authorities for their Christian activism, were seized under orders from the pagan ruler Duke Justus and sent to a prison in Armenia. Although they were never heard from again, there can be no doubt that they did not die of natural causes. The heart-broken Kyriaki, knowing that she was never to see her gentle parents again, insisted on carrying on their work despite the ever-increasing danger of her own capture. When she was finally taken into custody, she faced her captors with a calm courage and an assurance that puzzled the pagans.

Imprisoned in Nicomedia, she drew the attention of Maximilian, ruler of that area, who thought he could bend her will because of her youth and sex. He never made a greater mistake in judgment or was so wrong in the estimation of his power over the strength of Kyriaki's. Thwarted at every turn of his logic, and exasperated by her oratorical power, he ordered that Kyriaki be whipped in public. Bearing the punishment with great fortitude, she was then turned over to Ilarios, the governor of Bythnia.

It was at this point that the spark of divinity within Kyriaki asserted itself. Ordered to stand in a pagan temple to pray to their gods, she looked skyward, spread her arms, and called upon God to demonstrate His power over these malefactors. The reply terrified her enemies. A violent earthquake leveled the pagan temple, from which Kyriaki walked unscathed, and a bolt of lightning struck and killed Ilarios. God's wrath had been demonstrated, and when the pagans had overcome their shock, they decided that the only way to destroy this girl was by beheading her. This time Kyriaki merely prayed to God that her soul be taken before the executioner's axe could fall. This was the way Kyriaki died on July 7 at the age of twenty-one.

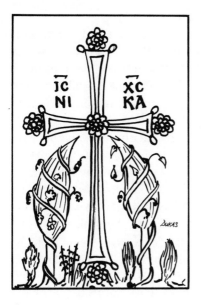

July 7

SS. Cyril and Methodios

One of the brightest chapters in the history of Christianity was recorded by two amazing brothers, whose missionary success in the Balkan countries (the Danubian region) stands forever as a monumental human endeavor. The awe-inspiring task of sowing the seeds of Christianity in so vast an area with two pairs of hands was a religious feat of strength unsurpassed by any who have labored for Christ. The architects of this awesome task were the brothers Cyril and Methodios, the Apostles to the Slavs.

Cyril, who was born Constantine, and his brother Methodios were two Greek brothers from Thessalonica. Methodios was born about A.D. 825, Constantine about A.D. 827. Both were scholars in the classical tradition, outstanding as intellectuals, theologians, and linguists. Cyril was a professor of philosophy at the patriarchal school in Constantinople and at one point took a leave of absence to participate in a mission among the Arabs. Methodios was the abbot of a Greek monastery when they decided to join in working for the conversion of the Khazars, northeast of the Black Sea. Their success in this joint effort brought them to the attention of the hierarchy, and they were encouraged to remain as a team in prospective programs for the spread of the Christian faith.

In 862, Rastislav, the ruler of Moravia, seeking to offset German political and religious pressures on the one hand and the influence of the Frankish kingdom on the other, sent to Constantinople for Orthodox support and missionaries. The Byzantine Emperor Michael III and the great Patriarch Photios entrusted the mission to the two brothers. In the following year they started their work among the Slavs, whose language they had mastered and put to use in all aspects of Church worship. In fact, historians maintain that the golden ages of the ninth and tenth centuries of the Church of Christ were brought about not only by the great Patriarch Photios but also by the two brothers, Cyril and Methodios. For this reason they were called the three "intellectual lamps" of that era.

With swift competence they established churches, taking care to use the Slavic tongue in the Liturgy and translating the Holy Scriptures into the language later known as Old Church Slavonic. They even invented a Slavonic alphabet based on Greek characters, which in its final form, Cyrillic, is still used by all Slavs belonging to the Eastern Orthodox Church. Sparing no effort, they brought about the complete Christian conversion of many Slavic peoples. Moreover, through a band of disciples they organized, the two brothers influenced the religious and cultural development of these people, evident to this day even behind the Iron Curtain.

Following this achievement, Cyril and Methodios accepted an invitation by Pope Nicholas to go to Rome to explain why they had used the Slavic tongue in the Liturgy. This practice was deplored by the German Archbishop of Salzburg and Bishop of Passau, who claimed control of the Slavic territory and the right to use the Latin Liturgy. By the time the brothers arrived in Rome, there was a new pope, Hadrian II, whose sympathies lay with the brothers and who therefore was in agreement with the Patriarch of Constantinople. He, too, authorized the use of the Slavic Liturgy.

The following year, Methodios was saddened by the death of his beloved brother and co-worker Cyril, and with a heavy heart agreed to serve the Slavs as Archbishop of Syrmium. The new ruler, Svatopluk, resented the influence of Methodios and conspired with others to have Methodios brought to trial before a German court in Bavaria. Methodios was kept in jail for three years during which he was brutally treated. At last liberated through the intervention of Pope John VIII, he sought Constantinople's assistance in the controversy over the use of the Slavic Liturgy, an issue which had still not been settled when Methodios died in 884. His death, however, did not end his work which was carried forward by his disciples in all Slavic lands. The feast of these remarkable brothers is observed on July 7.

St. Nikodemos
of the Holy Mountain

Of the countless devout monks who have served God and man on Mount Athos, one man's name has been synonymous with the Holy Mountain. He is remembered throughout Christendom as Nikodemos of the Holy Mountain. His distinguished record in the service of God reflected a divine gift in literature and music. With this gift he refined the age-old Church services and thus contributed in a rare way to the spiritual enhancement of Christian worshippers. His heaven-inspired genius was expressed eloquently in brief homilies and in more extensive works that are classics of Christian literature.

Born on the island of Naxos in the Cyclades of Greece in 1749, Nikodemos was a child prodigy who came to combine a remarkable intellect with an intimacy with God. In his continuous intellectual pursuits he found himself surpassing his instructors until he met Ierotheos, a man of philosophical wisdom and profound faith with whom Nikodemos studied in the city of Smyrna.

Nikodemos did not enter the monastery on Mount Athos until he was twenty-seven years of age. By this time he was superbly prepared for the great goals he had set for himself, which could be attained only within the confines of this magnificent cloister. His responsiblilities increased with his spiritual projects, and as secretary and official historian of the monastery he became a most prolific writer of theological prose. His prose works have become classics not only in theology, but also in literature as well. His pen added lustre to Christian worship and brought literary laurels to himself. He became a master of "wordship."

To supplement his references and to gather material for his many writings, he travelled to cities throughout Asia Minor and Eastern Europe, at times assisting local prelates in matters of interpretation and dogma.

In Moldavia he offered his translation of both the Old and New Testaments, and in Venice he set down his masterful Philokalia, drawing from the writing of holy men of the Church to form a spiritual guidebook that has become a standard text for clerics. With the precision of a mathematician, he compiled the holy canons, the rules of the Church, and a number of service books for the sacraments used by clergymen today. Among the many manuscripts that poured out of his inspired cornucopia is today's Confessions of Faith or Pedalion, which sets forth the canons and rules of the Church from the fourth century with such precision and clarity that it has been termed the "rudder" of the Church.

Equally gifted in music, Nikodemos composed the beautiful hymns heard in Church during the Holy Friday services of the funeral of Christ.

His masterpiece is a two volume edition of the "Lives of Saints," a spiritual and literary feat which flowed from his pen in a relatively short span of time and which is the authoritative reference on the saints of the first seventeen centuries of Christianity. In addition to compiling service books for the clergy, he set down in prose the life and times of St. Gregory Palamas, an interpretation of St. Paul, and a detailed calendar of the Church feast days. All of these works also won high acclaim in the Russian Orthodox and Roman Catholic Churches.

Beloved by all Christians whose lives have been enriched by this theological and literary giant and revered as one of the most gifted of its holy men, Nikodemos of the Holy Mountain died at the age of sixty on 14 July 1809.

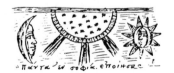

July 15

Vladimir (Basil) of Russia

Empire builder, statesman, soldier, leader, and ultimately an extraordinary missionary, Vladimir of Russia has been referred to by historians as nothing more than Prince Vladimir, but Christianity knows him as a saint, a title that exceeds that of "emperor" or "the great." The latter title, however, could have been accurately applied to Vladimir, a man who combined in his lifetime enough careers for an entire cabinet of ministers. His impressive credentials in secular life notwithstanding, it was his introduction of Christianity to a nation that was to swell in number to two hundred fifty million that placed him in the hallowed company of saints.

The son of Svyatoslav I, ruler of a fragmented Russia, Vladimir was born in Kiev in A.D. 972. With the death of his father, Vladimir fully expected to take over the reins of government but instead was forced into exile by powerful enemies. Taking refuge in Scandinavia, he secretly organized an army. With considerable daring and military skill, he put his enemies to flight and firmly established himself as Prince of Russia.

A pagan since birth, Vladimir saw the need for a common religion among his people that could assure a genuine unification. To that end he sent emissaries to Constantinople, Germany and the Moslem countries with directions to report what they could about the respective religions. The Russian monk, Nestor, records the report of the observer of the Moslems that "There was no gladness among them, only sorrow and a great stench; their religion is not a good one." The observer in Germany saw "no beauty" in the Latin ritual.

But in Constantinople, where the full festive ritual of the Orthodox Church was unveiled in all its splendor, the emissaries wrote back to Vladimir "we no longer knew whether we were in Heaven or on earth, for such beauty we know not how to tell of it." The news elated Vladimir, who himself had been greatly attracted to Orthodoxy and Byzantine civilization.

In the course of his introduction to Christianity, Vladimir also wanted to marry the sister of the Emperor Basil, who saw in this marriage a way of making an ally of this powerful ruler of the north. Soon after he was baptized, taking the name of the Emperor Basil, Vladimir and Basil's sister Anna were married and returned to Kiev. Christianity transformed Vladimir from pagan wretchedness to God's glorious love, and he plunged into the formidable task of bringing the word of Christ into the hearts of all the people of his country. By word of mouth and courier, the only media of the day, it took a great deal of skill, determination, and missionary zeal to see that the darkened reaches of the country were illuminated with the love of Christ.

Into an area larger than Europe, Vladimir untiringly applied himself to establishing not only churches, but schools, seminaries, convents, monasteries, and every form of Christian expression. The logistics of such an undertaking are breathtaking and required not only the skill of an able administrator, but the zeal of an apostle who had pledged himself to the spiritual enlightenment of an entire country. This great work culminated in the erection in A.D. 989 of the "Cathedral of the Tithes," which symbolized the great Christian zeal of Vladimir and his countrymen who came to call their ruler the "St. Paul of Russia."

The work of Christianizing Russia was facilitated by the use of the Slavic alphabet (invented by the great Greek missionaries SS. Cyril and Methodios) into which the gems of Christian literature were translated.

Prince Vladimir died in A.D. 1015 with the whole of Russia as his legacy to the Christian faith, which, despite Communism, to this day sees to the spiritual needs of the Christian community. The Father of his country as well as its Church, Prince Vladimir, whose gravesite has witnessed many miracles, was proclaimed a saint of the Church and accorded the rare title of "Isapostolos," equal to the Apostles.

July 22

St. Mary Magdalene

The doctrine of equal rights for women is not a twentieth century concept, but had its beginning with Jesus of Nazareth who accepted Mary Magdalene into His confidence and recognized her as being on equal footing with the Apostles. Such was the status of Mary Magdalene, who was privileged to walk beside our Savior, that she was bestowed with the title of "Isapostolos," "equal to the Apostles," a title of which few are aware. This ignorance of the true Mary Magdalene resulted from conflicting and misleading facts about her life, which diminished the true greatness of a woman who was favored by God to the extent that she had the confidence and companionship of Jesus Christ Himself.

The popular misconception that Mary Magdalene was a fallen woman stemmed from accounts of Western Christendom. It was assumed that since Mary came from Magdala, a city as notorious as Sodom and Gomorrah, she was of ill-repute and was later cleansed of her many sins by the Lord. On the contrary, the Evangelist Luke depicted her as the stricken woman whom Jesus healed by removing seven demons from within her. Be that as it may, it is universally known that following her confrontation with the Lord she rose to become His close friend and devoted follower.

What woman, fallen or not, would not have traded places with Mary Magdalene to be near Him who died to save the world, to be the woman who agonized at His trial, wept at His crucifixion, and glorified in His Resurrection? What greater honor than to be at the tomb of Christ and to speak to him (John 20: 1-18)? What Christian woman would not wish herself a Mary Magdalene to know the excitement of accompanying

St. John the Theologian after the Ascension of Christ?

The Biblical account of Mary Magdalene, like any passage from Scripture, must be read more than once, for in it will be found inspiration for Christian women who can identify with Mary. Aside from the Apostles themselves, none of our saints shared Mary's joy in being in Jesus' company. Other saints who were born at a later time did share an intimacy with the Lord while they were on earth, but Mary was alive when Jesus walked the earth.

How long Mary Magdalene lived after the death of Christ is not known, but what is certain is that she died in Ephesos where she had gone with St. John the Theologian. She was buried at the entrance to a cave where Christians had sought refuge. In the year A.D. 890 through painstaking research under the direction of Emperor Leo, the remains of Mary Magdalene were located, removed from the entrance of the cave and were transferred to the capital city of Constantinople. Her remains were buried in a chapel where the remains of Lazaros are also said to be buried.

Accorded the honor of being one of the Myrrh-bearing Women of the New Testament, Mary Magdalene was further honored with the grand title of "Isapostolos," a solemn tribute to a woman who had brought glory to all women of faith.

July 22

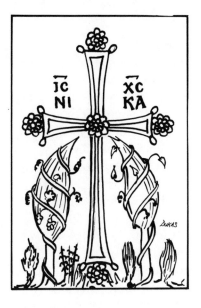

St. Marcella of Chios

On the small but pleasant island of Chios a chapel marks the sacred spot where a pretty Greek maiden, who saw no visions nor felt any divine presence, met a martyr's death in a most bizarre fashion. The divine nature of her life devoted to Christ came to light only after she had been slain not by enemies of the Church, but by the hand of her own irreligious and demented father. However, the tragic circumstances of her brutal end are overshadowed by the miraculous manifestations that ensued thereafter.

Born in the 16th century, Marcella of Chios possessed great physical beauty, exceeded only by the purity of her spirit and sweet soul. Her family was one of prominence on the island and she was given every advantage, including that available to anyone — a place in the Kingdom of God through Jesus Christ. The entire island soon came to know the intensity of her religious beliefs, but no one was the least bit aware of the divine spark in this pretty Greek girl. Her closeness to God went undetected as she prayed with the townspeople in Church and in her daily meditations in contemplation of the Holy Spirit.

After the death of her devout mother, Marcella withdrew from social pursuits in order to completely devote herself to the service of Christ, choosing to emerge from seclusion only for Church attendance and for whatever charitable work she could do for the community. It can be concluded that she did not seek the sanctity of a nunnery out of great fear of her father, who had become increasingly irritated by her complete devotion to Christ. An avowed agnostic, her father's mental state worsened gradually until he was socially unacceptable because of his aberrations. He vented his feelings of anger and frustration by heaping abuse upon his daughter, whom he came to see as the cause of all his troubles.

The deteriorating mental condition of Marcella's father caused her as much concern for his health as for her own safety. In trying to reason him into a relatively calm demeanor, she found herself threatened with dire punishment. Given over to complete madness, the father raged at the daughter in such a torrent of abuse that she fled from the house, taking to the hills. This action so enraged the madman that he followed in hot pursuit. While seeking a hiding place, Marcella fell between two rocks and became wedged between them, helpless before the vengeful maniac who killed his own child on the spot.

While still mourning the death of the pious Marcella, an islander visited the site of the fateful rocks where she died. There he made the startling discovery that water was exuding from between these rocks where there had been none before. Soon the entire island came to know that not only was there water coming from the spot but that it contained miraculous powers of healing. The community then reassessed the piety of the beautiful Marcella and with the conviction that she was a true martyr, they erected a chapel as a shrine to her loving memory.

Islanders tell the story that the rocks in the immediate area of the sacred site have turned blood red, and in some instances quite black, as though symbolic of the blood of the martyrs of Christianity. Pilgrimages to this site have continued unabated ever since the discovery; particularly on July 22, the day on which Marcella met death, are pilgrimages made to this shrine. This divine manifestation is unique principally because Marcella was not the typical homespun, poor peasant girl, but rather a beautiful, aristocratic, and highly intelligent girl. Furthermore, although her Christian zeal was made evident through various overt acts of Christian charity and belief, she was of no religious order, nor the favorite of any recognized religious authority. But there is no question that this girl had an intimacy with God which is evidenced by the miraculous occurrence at the site where she was murdered by a father whom she might have placated with a disavowal of Christ.

SAINT

PANTELEIMON

Δ. Dukas

*St. Panteleimon
(The All-Merciful)*

A man whose life span was four years shorter than the Savior whom he served crammed into his twenty-nine years on earth enough achievement in science and religion to fill the entire fourth century. Like the great St. Luke of the New Testament, Panteleimon was a doctor and was referred to reverently as "a glorious physician." Unlike Luke, Panteleimon attained sainthood not through his evangelism, but through his talents as a physician whose efforts on behalf of the suffering were augmented by the power of the divine.

Panteleimon the All-Merciful was born in A.D. 275 in Nicomedia, Asia Minor, of a pagan father and a Christian mother. From his father he derived a profound intellect; from his mother, spiritual awareness. Together they provided him with the skill and dedication that were to thrust him into prominence, then into tragedy within a relatively short span of time. Of handsome appearance and noble bearing, Panteleimon was an impressive figure while still a student of the Empire's most noted physician, Euphrosinos, a teacher who took pride in his pupil's remarkable skill and dedication.

He had not been a physician long when his reputation as a healer drew him to the attention of Emperor Maximilian, who encouraged him with his personal sponsorship. This quickly led to Panteleimon's recognition as the foremost physician of the entire known world. Panteleimon became a familiar figure among the people as he went from one patient to another while yet serving the Emperor and his court. The demand for his services kept him working at a feverish pace, an exhausting obligation he never shirked.

In the course of his rounds he had been observed by the pious Christian Ermolaos, one who remained in constant hiding in fear of persecution by the State for his overt promotion of Christianity. Ermolaos managed to intercept Panteleimon, whose great skill he lauded but who he thought needed to be reminded "from the most high cometh healing." After a series of meetings the physician came to know his true Christian destiny, and thereafter his professionalism as a man of medicine was subordinated to his role as a healer in the name of the greatest healer of them all. His power of healing was not attributable to a physician's skill alone, but to divine intervention as well. As his reputation grew, Panteleimon came to be known more as a man of God than of science, an acknowledgment that brought wrath and cruel action by the Emperor.

After being given the customary interrogation Panteleimon was offered the ultimate choice between Christ and the idols; his response was a reaffirmation of his Christianity. For the noble physician it was a two-edged sword: first because he was a fallen favorite whose betrayal was a personal rebuke to the Emperor, and secondly because of the steadfastness of his loyalty to the Savior.

Not all of the fiendish designs of Panteleimon's torture are known, but history tells us that this honorable doctor and noble Christian was, among other things, stretched across a rack and burned by candles. Following this ordeal he was cast first into a fiery pit and then into a den of beasts. When he survived the pagans were convinced he had the protection of some kind of sorcery. It was finally decided that since there could be no antidote for drowning, he would be cast into a deep river with a huge stone bound to his body. When the stone proved buoyant, the exasperated torturers fished him out of the water and placed him on the execution block where he was beheaded.

It was said that not blood but milk flowed from the severed head of the martyr. Panteleimon gave his life for Christ on 27 July 304.

July 30

St. Julitta

One of the strongholds of Christianity in the fourth century was the city of Cappadocia, in Asia Minor, which gave a world plunged in spiritual darkness the bright light of some of Christ's most illustrious figures. The brilliance of a woman named Julitta was such that a fellow Cappadocian, the great St. Basil, saw fit to praise her in poetry as a Christian of rare spirit and magnificent courage. Through the acknowledgment of St. Basil and other luminaries, this pious woman gained the recognition which culminated in sainthood.

While the details of the early life of Julitta remain obscure, it is known that she was born into a family of great wealth and prominence. She was raised in an atmosphere of spiritual as well as material abundance. Her family was devoutly Christian, despite the fact that it was not fashionable in those days to profess faith in the humble Carpenter. Christianity was regarded by the more affluent as the religion of the oppressed and the downtrodden. Whenever any one of means emerged as a Christian, his choice of Christ was not arrived at easily, and he invariably was a most devout follower.

While still comparatively young Julitta found herself sole heiress to a fortune which was comprised largely of land holdings with ill-defined boundaries and herds that roamed far and wide under the care of countless slaves. The overseer could keep accurate account of the granaries and storehouses, but a headcount of stock would have been equivalent to taking a census, so vast and scattered were the flocks. It was the lack of exact boundaries, usually maintained on an honor system, which was to afford her enemies the opportunity to take unfair advantage of this woman of God.

Dedicating all her efforts to the development of the Church, Julitta's only active role in the estate was to insure that the slaves, who could not be freed without arousing suspicion, were treated like other employees and were secretly paid for their efforts. Aside from that she cared little for the estate, except to see that the proceeds were directed to the Church and to the care of the needy.

The neighboring landowners began gradually to encroach upon the territory that had been in Julitta's family for years. Others were motivated to proclaim squatters rights so that in due time Julitta found her little empire all but illegally overrun by pagan despoilers. Their envy for her holdings and her Christian piety was intensified by the fact that her earnings were given over to the poor and to her Christian Church. She soon found herself driven to bring suit lest her entire estate be devoured by these pagans.

Before the magistrate was paraded a motley array of witnesses, all of whom bore false testimony against Julitta in an effort to discredit her. Given a set of circumstances such as those invented by her neighbors, a Christian's property might be held forfeit. To the surprise of the presiding magistrate, Julitta professed that her only regret was that the Church and the poor would be deprived of the financial assistance but that the Lord would not forsake them. She declared that the forfeiting of her property would be equivalent to sealing their own fate, since the spirit of Christ would prevail over their lifeless, spiritual idols. She reasserted her faith in God and urged them to come into Christ's fold before it was too late. She held sway for several minutes until finally one of the pagans demanded that she be silenced.

The Roman magistrate was not moved by Julitta's impassioned pleas in the name of Christ. On the contrary, he considered her exhortation to be an insult to the gods, and without delay he ordered her to be put to death. History relates that the pagans cast her into a fiery pit. Julitta gave her life for Christ on July 30.

August 7

St. Theodosios of Argos

D. Δukaʃ

When St. Paul stood on Mars Hill in the ancient city of Athens exhorting the assembled Hellenes to renounce their pagan idols and accept Jesus Christ as the Son of God, his voice was to echo down through the corridors of time to reach the ears of a Greek more than 800 years later, who himself was to become a revered saint of the Christian faith. Out of the thousands whose ancestors stood before the mighty St. Paul on the bleak hill that faces the Acropolis, it was Theodosios who seems to have been endowed with a divine spark equal with his given name.

Born in A.D. 862 in an era when the Christian Church was firmly established and had proved to be the light of a world slowly emerging from the spiritual shadows. Theodosios was born into a family of devout adherents of Orthodox worship. His early training was in the highest tradition of the Christian faith, and at an early age he resolved to give himself over completely to the service of Christ to take up his life's work in a region of the rugged Peloponnesos near the town of Argos.

While en route to this area, Theodosios had a vision in which St. John the Baptist appeared and directed him to build a chapel named after him and for which he would receive the blessing of St. John, in the name of Jesus. Enlisting the aid of the faithful, Theodosios saw to the completion of this beautiful chapel, and thereafter, filled with the heavenly spirit, sought a life of monasticism so that he might draw nearer to God through meditation and prayer. Many years passed before he turned once again to the company of man, and it was soon evident that he had been blessed with the ability to heal through the power of Jesus. Those who sought his comfort and healing saw in him the divine grace of his patron, St. John the Baptist, and a trace of the serenity of Jesus.

The monastery that Theodosios nurtured to a haven of prominence attracted pilgrims from all the regions of Christianity and was never to know the threat of persecution. Its huge success was to stir envy within the hearts of some who sought to discredit him. Their petty jealousy of this holy man led to accusations of witchcraft and sorcery. When they branded him a heretic, a clamor grew that caused Archbishop Petros, who innocently had accepted the evil distortions of the detractors of Theodosios, to consider a reprimand.

While contemplating what disciplinary action to take against Theodosios, the Archbishop of Argos was summoned to an Ecumenical council at the Patriarchate. While travelling to Constantinople, the Archbishop dreamt one night that Theodosios admonished him for accepting unfounded charges against him. At the same time, the Patriarch received a similar dream in which Theodosios protested his innocence of any wrongdoing. When the Archbishop and the Patriarch discovered that they had experienced the same dream, and about the same time, they accepted it as divine proof of the innocence of Theodosios.

Upon his return to Argos, the Archbishop went directly to Theodosios, relating what had happened and expressing his regret for having considered the idea of disciplinary measures against him. The Archbishop's endorsement of Theodosios put the envy to rest and put an end to any doubt regarding Theodosios' nearness to God. Thus exonerated, and with the support of the Archbishop, Theodosios continued with his holy work until his death on 7 August 921. The chapel of St. John the Baptist still stands in Argos, Peloponnesos.

August 14

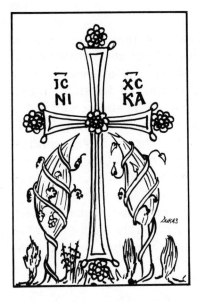

Marcellos of Apamea, Syria

The island of Cyprus in the eastern Mediterranean has been the scene of what seemed to have been everlasting turmoil, with a history of occupation by various conquerors since the days of the Roman Empire. The resulting political and religious turbulence in Cyprus has been such that it is a wonder that the island has not deteriorated into a wasteland and has survived at all. The island's occupants, realizing the strategic importance of their island, have taken pride through the centuries in being called Cypriots and have staunchly survived conquest and upheaval. A man who later became a saint while in another country, Marcellos of Apamea, Syria, was one of the island's illustrious ones.

Marcellos was born into a wealthy and socially prominent Cypriot family. He was reared in an atmosphere of privilege and political favor, receiving the utmost in education since his family hoped to prepare him for government service. From the outset it appeared that Marcellos' career would be purely political; thus no thought was given to his religious training. Active in civic affairs, Marcellos showed such qualities of leadership that Emperor Theodosios appointed him governor of the island.

While serving the state, Marcellos felt himself drawn to an even greater calling. Each month he withdrew more and more from the affairs of state; he attended more and more closely to the affairs of his heart which urged him to serve Christ. Resigning his office, he studied for his ministry with a dedication that carried him to the heights of Christendom. Not long after his ordination he was consecrated Bishop of Apamea in Syria, a country which was in great need of a religious leader as noble as Marcellos. He brought the promise of Christ to a land spiritually deceived by cults, sorcery, and superstition.

Marcellos undertook the formidable task of converting this array of heathens with great enthusiasm and devotion. In a relatively brief span of time the skeletal Christian group he had found huddled in obscurity flourished with a steady wave of newcomers accepting the Messiah. The leadership qualities which Marcellos had developed as governor of Cyprus were now employed even more forcefully and productively in the service of Christ. Yet his very success was to spell his own doom.

It was a common practice at this time for Christian converts to attack their former places of worship. Thus, under Marcellos' leadership the zealous converts destroyed the pagan temples and the idols which they had worshipped only a short time before. In reaction to Marcellos' campaign against paganism, the remaining pagans travelled to the main temple of Syria, where the god Zeus was worshipped, to take a stand against the Christians.

Marcellos and his followers stacked vessels of holy water against the formidable pagan temple and called upon God to destroy it. While praying for this divine intervention, Marcellos and his friends looked up to see the temple engulfed by flames. Unseen pagans seized Marcellos and cast him into the flames; the conflagration that destroyed the pagan abomination also took the life of a man who glorified God. Marcellos died a martyr on 14 August 460.

August 19

St. Theophanes of Mt. Athos

Had it not been for the practice of exhuming one's remains after three years, a common practice in Greece because usable soil is so precious, Theophanes of Mt. Athos might never have been venerated as a saint. It was not until his earthly remains had been unearthed that he was discovered to have a likeness to the divine. In his lifetime his intimacy with God, evident through his dedication to the spirit of Christ, assured him a place in Church history among the spiritually great men and women of Christianity. Yet, it was not until after his death that his true greatness came to light.

During the seventeenth century, at a time when Greece was still plagued by her Turkish conquerors, Theophanes was born in the picturesque city of Ioannina where he also received his education. He was reared by devout parents in an atmosphere of love for Christ and his fellow man, teachings which he made evident throughout his lifetime. While still a youth he felt the call to monasticism and with credentials that showed him to be destined for spiritual greatness he was admitted to a monastery on Mt. Athos.

Theophanes progressed through the ranks of these holy men with unusual advancement, solely on his own merits, and soon he was elected abbot — this honor was later set aside in order to save a man's life. Shortly after his ascension to the directorship of Athos, he was informed by his sister that her son had been taken prisoner by the Turks and was facing possible torture and perhaps even death. He did not hesitate to put the life of his nephew above the glory of his office, and left word that if he succeeded in saving his nephew, he would not bring him back to Mt. Athos lest the monastery itself be threatened by the Turks.

Theophanes traveled to Constantinople where he contacted sources close to the state and asked them to arrange his nephew's escape. Despite the great risk, Theophanes' friends completed the escape and safe return of his nephew to Greece. Forced to forsake his post on Mt. Athos, Theophanes selected a site in Macedonia, just outside the city, where he founded a monastery and a chapel dedicated to St. John the Baptist. Afterwards, he established another monastery in the name of the Archangels, located within the limits of the city of Naousa, a community whose magnificent waterfalls and abundant fruit groves provided a proper setting for the solemn spiritual work of the monks.

When death approached him, Theophanes summoned his fellow monks, all of whom assured him that his work would be carried on with the same excellence that he had assumed throughout his lifetime of service to God. Theophanes died on 19 August 1690. Respected in life, he was greatly revered by those who came to pay their respects. Although some prayers that had been offered at his burial site were answered, these were not taken seriously until he was exhumed after the customary three-year waiting period.

The skull of Theophanes was placed in the chapel of the Archangels. Once there, miraculous healing powers were manifested by touching the skull of this holy man. So great in number were these manifestations that Theophanes was afterwards made a saint in the Orthodox Church. The city of Naousa was destroyed by the Turks during the Greek War of Independence in 1822. It has since been restored, even to the waterfalls and fruit groves, as a reminder that Theophanes lost his Mt. Athos position to save his nephew, but found eternity in a village which now honors him as a saint.

August 26

St. Joasaph

It is rather unusual that the land of India, with its many intrigues plus the cults that have over the centuries all but crowded out the hardy Christians who dwell there, would give one of its most illustrious sons to the cause of Christianity. Even St. Thomas, one of the twelve Apostles, was drawn to this fascinating land and has come to be known as the patron saint of India. It remained for an Indian prince, however, to symbolize the Christian spirit there.

In the time of Constantine the Great, a proud monarch called Abenner ruled over what we now know as India. He was highly respected for his courage as a warrior and esteemed for his administrative wisdom. His intense passion for the Indian code of honor was exceeded only by his fierce hatred of Christianity. The Christian code of piety, forgiveness and love for Christ was an offense to this king who considered the Christian code to be that of weakness. He failed to see the quiet courage of the Christians whom he ordered to be put to death.

When the queen bore the king a son, whom he joyously named Joasaph, the entire royal court was summoned to pay homage to the young prince. In keeping with the custom, the royal astrologers prophesied that young Joasaph would become a mighty monarch. There was one dissenting voice among the astrologers, however. One dared to foresee that the heir to the throne would, on the contrary, forsake it for Christianity. The king's answer to this was death or banishment for every Christian in the land. Not content with this, the distraught king had a huge castle erected in which he secluded his son for twenty years. The king afforded his son every luxury, educated him with all the wisdom at the command of his tutors, and pridefully watched the development of his son's mental and physical powers in an environment so insulated that he never knew Christianity existed.

Satisfied that the prediction of his son's conversion was completely false, and thinking that he had eliminated every trace of Christianity in his country, the father finally yielded to his son's ever-increasing desire to leave his sheltered environment and journey into the land of the people he would one day rule. Joasaph's great joy at being able to see for himself the marvels of this ancient land was quickly replaced with sadness at the sight of want, disease, and misery. When he returned to the castle the joyous sights did not elate him. Instead, he became determined to find his real purpose in life, which he felt could not be succession to his father's throne. On the very day the prince returned to his castle, a thousand miles from the castle the pious monk Barlaam heard the voice of God calling him to seek out Joasaph to bring him the light of the Savior. Barlaam made his way to India and gained access to the castle. Once there, the prince concealed him. With reverence and awe he listened while Barlaam revealed to him the true meaning of life in Jesus. Joasaph quickly found peace with God and was reborn through his baptism performed by Barlaam. Such was the strength of his new-found faith in God that he not only converted his entire household but in due course he was able to win over to the cause of Christ his father, who for so many years had stubbornly opposed Christianity.

After the death of the King, Joasaph ruled wisely and well but found no satisfaction in the monarchy. He longed for the company of Barlaam and for a complete dedication of his life in the service of Christ. Turning the rule of the government over to his family, Joasaph abdicated the power and the pomp of the throne for the simple monastery of the desert where he became a legend during his own lifetime. His feast day is celebrated on August 26.

Δ. Δukas

St. Moses the Ethiopian

During the fourth century a man of God transformed the brute Moses, a slave, to a crusader for Christ. The energies of this slave were averted from the path of evil to the path of righteousness with the result that he became a saint of the Orthodox Church. Prophetically this native of Abyssinia was given the name of Moses, but in his homeland and later in Ethiopia, the only thing he had in common with the Moses of the Old Testament was the bondage each endured. By the time he had reached maturity, this giant of a man, who possessed great strength, had gained the reputation of being a quick-tempered troublemaker. His yoke of slavery served only to stir the fierce passions within him. When his master was finally unable to bring the unruly Moses into line with his more obedient slaves, he ordered his release.

With hatred still seething in him, Moses took to the desert but found no pleasure in his freedom. Forced to care for himself, Moses preyed on others and formed a band of robbers with recruits from every den of thieves in the Middle East. With his motley group of misfits and unbelievers, he terrorized the countryside with his daring raids until the alarmed citizens pleaded for aid from the state. The troops were no match for the cunning Moses, and the brutality continued at full force to the extent that travelers would not enter the areas where Moses had been reported. His notoriety even came to be celebrated in songs which told of his daring and great strength.

As he came upon a monastery, his provisions were running low, and with no regard for its accepted immunity, he decided to plunder the monastery. He burst in upon the abbot, fully expecting that he would cower as all others had at the sight of his scowling face. But it was Moses, not the abbot, who was surprised by the sudden encounter. The holy man, far from being alarmed, simply stood there with a quiet composure and gazed directly into the eyes of the motionless intruder. At that moment, Moses felt the disturbing resentment he had harbored for years begging to leave him. The bitterness that had resulted in violence was gone; Moses began to experience something he never felt before — regret, which in turn became contrition. He disbanded his band and asked to be allowed to stay and a-chieve the fulfillment of what he now recognized to be his real purpose in life.

He spent many hours with the kindly abbot, confessing all his sins and asking him to pray for the forgiveness of his transgressions. When he had at last satisfied himself that he could make up for the misdeeds of his past, he took up residence as a monk. He was determined to right every wrong he had committed and to bring the light of Christ which he had received from the pious abbot to those who did not have it. The gnawing defiance was replaced by a serenity that he had never known, allowing him to redirect his boundless energy from its previous course to one that would carry him to the throne of the Savior.

The name of Moses that had struck terror in the hearts of men of the Middle East soon came to bring comfort to the oppressed and downtrodden; the troop of bandits that had plundered became an army of Christian monks that he headed to bring the word of Christ to every corner of the eastern Empire. After organizing followers that numbered in the thousands, he retired to the desert, where he founded one of the greatest monasteries of the fourth century. By the time of his death he had seventy disciples preaching the word of Christ throughout the Middle East. He lived to be eighty-five and unlike most saints of the Church who lived in peace and died in violence, Moses, who had lived his early life in violence, died in peace shortly before A.D. 400.

SAINT THE
SYMEON STYLITE
Dukas

September 1

St. Symeon Stylites

There have been men who could call forth enthusiasm for Christ from the pulpit, or from monastic cells, but for forty long years one man did so perched atop a sixty foot pillar from which he never descended. He spent a lifetime of extreme asceticism that spelled out the name of the Savior twenty-four hours of every day of that long period. In a stint of religious fervor that has been imitated many times since but never duplicated, St. Symeon occupied a confining space above ground. Like a wingless eagle of the Lord, he made a spectacular figure against the sky that reminded everyone below that the only salvation of man could come through Jesus Christ.

In his youth, Symeon was an earthbound shepherd who had deep Christian roots originating in the Syrian city of Antioch, the first city to apply the name "Christian" to the followers of Jesus of Nazareth. Such was the depth of his faith that it could find expression only through asceticism. This austerity through monastic life he was to carry to the extreme not only to completely dedicate himself to God, but to call to the attention of the world the need for prayer in Christian worship.

At a time when St. Anthony and St. Savvas were gaining their reputation through monasticism in Egypt, Symeon chose to carry out his ascetic way of life in his native Syria, a land where monastics had been dwarfed by the spiritual giants of other areas. This relative obscurity might have generated his brilliant idea to ascend the pillar, located about sixteen miles from the city of Aleppo on a road leading to Antioch. This was, however, no mere publicity-seeking flagpole stunt. It was a well thought-out plan to present the appealing starkness of a lone figure's vigil for Christ with the bare necessities of life being provided by devoted followers. His self-denial was subordinate to the main purpose of his thought-provoking venture, which was to bring his fellow man an acute awareness of and a closer proximity to God. In this he was eminently successful, a price in deprivation he was only too glad to pay.

Symeon's severely restricted abode, in which he could either stand or sit but could not lie down, limited his physical movement, but that seemed only to give him more room for intellectual effort, prayer and meditation. Known as a stylite, or one who lives on a pillar, he virtually impaled himself physically for a lifetime but thereby gained spiritual eternity. Inured to the hardships of this inhuman existence, he was able to withstand rigors which by any standard would be unbearable, and it is not hard to believe that in one Lenten season he stood erect for twenty days, then sat in meditation for another twenty days, during which time his only sustenance was water.

Considered to be by far the greatest hermit in all Christendom, Symeon sat or stood stoically atop his pillar, which over the years beckoned thousands of Christian pilgrims who came to view this amazing spectacle and to hear the wisdom of the solitary anchorite, whose weather-beaten visage inspired countless numbers to reaffirm their faith in God and His only begotten Son. Added to the wonder of his durability under the most demanding circumstances was his power of miraculous healing through the power of the Lord, as a result of which he came to be venerated as a saint while still alive. Symeon had spent a number of years in his cramped quarters when he was besieged by his followers to descend back into the society of man, assuring him that his purpose had been more than fulfilled and that he was entitled to the comforts of hearth and home, even perhaps a high post in the hierarchy. Symeon refused to come down, saying only he had made a solemn vow that his only descent would come after his death. At various intervals, he would be reminded that he had earned his place in God's scheme of things, but on being refused every time, the good Christians below gave up trying to make Symeon change his mind.

The ruins of Symeon's pillar are still evident in Syria and are considered a shrine to the greatest ascetic of them all who died in A.D. 459 after establishing a precedent which many have followed but none has equalled.

September 3

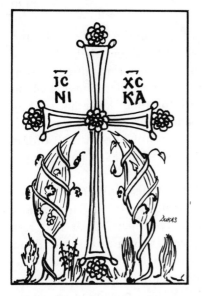

Anthimos of Nikomedia

Not unlike many other jewels of the Byzantine period was the ancient city of Nicomedia on the shores of the Sea of Marmara in Asia Minor. A spectacularly beautiful array of gleaming buildings, broad agoras, and plush gardens was created by the Nicomedes of Bythnia. Such was the glamor of this urban center that it was made the chief city of Diocletian and for that reason enjoyed immense popularity, to the dismay and envy of many other metropolitan areas. Christianity first took hold there during the reign of the Roman Emperor Maximianus. It was in this small but progressive Christian community that a man named Anthimos was to serve Christ to the degree that he became a saint.

Anthimos was an earnest and fearless priest of a Christian church at a time when Christianity was being attacked from all sides by the pagan majority who were confirmed by those unfortunates who had not heard the message of Christ. It was to the latter more than to the former that Anthimos directed his efforts. He had already earned a reputation for Christian piety and devotion when the triumphant Emperor Maximianus returned to the city following his conquest of Ethiopia.

Flushed with his great victory, the Emperor proclaimed a holiday period of celebration, and in conjunction with that he instructed his subjects to give thanks and pay homage to the pagan gods whose favor he had won. However, the Christians, who had grown in numbers, defied that order under the leadership of Anthimos, who was now their bishop. When he received word of this, the Emperor ordered that their church be destroyed by fire and that the worshippers of Jesus be put to death.

Anthimos was forewarned by a friend in the king's circle, and gathering his flock, he took to the hills, from where they saw the sky light up from their blazing church. Undaunted, Anthimos and his people pressed on to a town called Simanis where they rested and thanked the Lord for their deliverance. They were given little time, however, and their rejoicing was short-lived. The soldiers of the king were in hot pursuit with orders to capture Bishop Anthimos and return him in chains to royal justice.

Anthimos made the task easier for his pursuers for at his bidding they were told where he could be found. The soldiers were astounded when Anthimos asked them to sit and rest and share his simple food. The gentle Bishop assured them that he would cooperate with them to the fullest; meanwhile they were to rest up for the long journey back to the city. They were so overcome with shame for enchaining so gentle a priest that they offered to return without him on the pretext that their quarry had eluded them. The smiling Anthimos assured them that their truthfulness was worth more than the risk of being punished for their failure.

Suffice it to say that all the soldiers who had pursued Anthimos were soon converted to Christianity. Cast into prison, Anthimos was put to unspeakable torture, but throughout his suffering not once did he flinch in his allegiance to Christ. He was beheaded on 7 September 307.

September 4

St. Hermione

A little known heroine of the Christian Faith, Hermione was the daughter of one of Christ's Apostles. Although she might have made her way to heaven on the coattails of her father, she not only made it on her own, but became a saint herself. Her father was Philip, who at the time of his calling had four daughters. All four daughters of St. Philip were very beautiful and quite talented but of the four, only Hermione was to follow in her father's footsteps.

According to church records, after her father's death, Hermione journeyed to Asia Minor to find John, the one remaining Apostle of the original twelve. But John, who had been preaching at Ephesos when Hermione left her home, died before she could reach him, the only one of the twelve to die a peaceful death. Hermione then resolved to labor in the vineyard of Christ in the tradition of her father.

In 105 she took up the challenge for Christ by working with a highly respected clergyman, a missionary named Petronius, whose reputation for pious zeal was already established. It was then that Hermione's skill as a physician was discovered and with the help of Petronius, she concentrated on the care of the sick and the handicapped. During this time Hermione also began to display the power of prophecy. Her uncanny predictions consistently proved accurate and thus she acquired renown throughout the Roman Empire as a healer and prophet.

On his way to Ephesos to engage the Persians in combat, the Emperor Trajan, who had heard of Hermione's gifts and had attributed them to some kind of sorcery, summoned her before him. Thinking her talents might be put to his own useful purpose, he insisted that she accompany him in his quest for world domination. When she adamantly refused, he had her flogged in the public square and left her in disgust.

After the death of Trajan, his successor Hadrian summoned Hermione to his court to pass sentence on her. The smoldering envy which he had for Hermione before assuming the throne flared up and he alleged that she had committed various crimes against the state. Well aware of both her father's and her own Christian devotion, he prodded her with a barrage of questions about the legitimacy of her Faith. Finally he demanded that she denounce Christ or suffer punishment. When she refused, Hadrian had her tortured; when she courageously withstood the cruelty, he had her cast into prison, surrounded by several guards. While Hadrian was considering his next move, Hermione was quietly preaching to her captors. They were on the brink of conversion when the order came to place her in the pagan temple, there to be mocked by the pagan gods and the public. God answered Hermione's prayer by destroying the temple in a violent earthquake, whereupon the enraged ruler sent Hermione back to her captors while he planned her death.

By then the guards had been completely won over to the Christian faith. In one of the most remarkable turnabouts in Church history they whisked their captive away to the safety of the surrounding hills. So committed were they to her safekeeping that the irate Emperor was never able to find any trace of either Hermione or of the guards who had defied him and had converted to Christianity.

Thus, although Hermione had faced certain agonizing death, she was spared so that she might live out her life in peace. When death did come to Hermione, she was in the company of the faithful Christians whom she had converted. After she departed from this life, they carried on her holy work in her memory as well as that of her father.

Δ. Δukaς

September 11

Efrosynos the Cook

Although the paths of righteousness that may lead any
Christian to sainthood are
many in number, they do not
contain any directional signs,
nor are they limited in access
to any particular class of
individuals. These holy ranks
of men and women come from
all stations in life, from the
weak and the strong, the humble and the mighty, the simple
and the scholarly. God shows no favoritism and accepts among
the saints those who served Him best regardless of their back-
ground or extraction.

While Mt. Athos has been a spiritual haven for some of the
greatest minds in Church history, it has also opened its doors
to those of limited intellect whose devotion to God was limit-
less. Their power was more spiritual than intellectual. Among
these children of God who had no academic credentials was
a peasant named Efrosynos, who was admitted to the monastery
of Mt. Athos for his pure and simple spirit. His illiterate but
devout parents had given him no formal schooling, but had
enriched his life through devout prayer.

Unqualified for any sort of intellectual work, Efrosynos
was relegated to the kitchen. There he performed the menial
but not necessarily demeaning work of preparing the meals.
For this reason he was called Efrosynos the Cook. While many
have looked down their intellectual noses at the cook, none
of the more educated monks ever doubted his sincerity. While
he dispensed food for the body, Efrosynos found food for
his soul.

When he was not in the kitchen, Efrosynos sought seclusion in one of the many caves in the area. There he meditated and prayed in his own way, thereby acquiring an intimacy with God for which many of the scholars would have traded their entire knowledge. It was to this seclusion that Efrosynos had crept after having attended a rather profound lecture and discussion of the Kingdom of Heaven, conducted by the abbot. He was able to comprehend very little and contributed little if anything to the discussion. Retiring in embarrassment and confusion, Efrosynos crept to his place of seclusion to address God Himself in his own simple terms.

In a dream one night the abbot envisioned a garden of breathtaking beauty. In the center of it stood a lone figure which he discerned to be none other than Efrosynos. Of the hundreds of monks of Mt. Athos, only the lowly cook occupied the garden. In the dream, Efrosynos explained to the incredulous abbot that he was looking upon the Kingdom of Heaven, and then placed a branch laden with apples in the abbot's hands and walked away into the mist.

When the abbot awoke from the dream, he found himself clutching a real branch with real apples. Excitedly he summoned Efrosynos and the other monks to share this revelation. The new-found respect and admiration of his fellow monks only made the cook ill-at-ease and so he excused himself to seek the seclusion he cherished, but now with the knowledge that he had somehow received God's favor. The apples the abbot found in his hand were said to have had miraculous powers, but Efrosynos himself never bothered to witness this. He left for his place of solitude, which he enjoyed to his last day. Efrosynos is depicted in icons as holding an apple branch in his hand . His memory is celebrated on September 11.

September 16

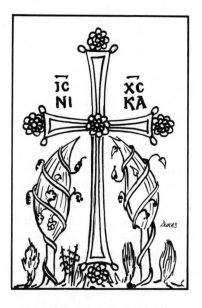

St. Euphemia the Martyr

The Patriarchate of Constantinople — that ancient city
which is now Istanbul — is
steeped in centuries-old tradition and is the guardian of
many ancient and holy relics.
Among these sacred relics are
those of one of the most
remarkable women in all ecclesiastical history, St. Eu-
phemia, the martyr. The story of the events of her glory-filled
life which culminated in sainthood would fill a good-sized book
if told in detail. Indeed, her influence on Christianity spanned
nearly two centuries.

Euphemia was born in Chalcedon, Asia Minor at the time
of Diocletian. Her parents, Philoform and Theodosian, belonged to the highest aristocracy of the day. Thus Euphemia
was reared in the grand manner befitting a young lady of her
station. Of noble intellect and high purpose, she could have
lived in splendor and luxurious ease, but she chose a more serious way of life. A true believer in Christ, she devoted herself
to the physical and spiritual welfare of those Christians less
fortunate than herself.

Her complete immersion in the cause of Christ was an abomination to the provincial governor, Priscus, especially because
her noble birthright demanded that she share the governor's
scorn for Christians. Seeking to strengthen his position, Priscus
ordered the arrest of Euphemia and ordered the high priest of
the pagan temple, Apellanian, to bring their apostate back to
worship in the temple of Aris. Had this been accomplished the
consequences would have been harmful to the Christian community, but Euphemia never wavered. Tenaciously she clung to
her Christian faith. Imprisoned, berated, and tortured to no
avail, she was finally thrown into the arena to be devoured

for the amusement of the pagan populace. She met her violent end on 16 September 305.

The anticlimax of her story unfolded over 150 years after her death. In the year 451 a clergyman named Eutyches advanced the teaching that Jesus Christ, the Son of God, could not have had two natures — human and divine — because the human had been absorbed by the divine. This concept was in direct opposition to accepted dogma and constituted heresy. The belief that Christ was both fully God and fully man was thus challenged. This controversy concerning the nature of Christ was so great and the resulting confusion reached such proportions that the Empress Pulcheria convoked an Ecumenical Council in A.D. 451. This Council resolved once and for all the accuracy of the Orthodox teaching on the dual nature of Christ.

During this council the holy relics of St. Euphemia witnessed to the truth that Christ was both God and man. The council had been convened in Chalcedon, where the Chapel of St. Euphemia was located. While the members of the Council were in Chalcedon, they witnessed miracles of healing attributed to the relics of St. Euphemia. Before this time her relics had not been recognized as miracle-working.

Someone proposed that the writing of Eutyches concerning the nature of Christ be placed in the casket of St. Euphemia alongside those of the Fathers of the Church. They closed the casket and after a period of silent prayer reopened it. The heretical works of Eutyches were found at the feet of St. Euphemia and the Orthodox writings of the Fathers were clutched in her arms. Thus the fate of Eutyches was confirmed. His teachings were condemned and the Orthodox doctrine of the dual nature of Christ was firmly established. Shortly thereafter, the remains of St. Euphemia were transferred to the Ecumenical Patriarchate in Constantinople, where she lies in honored glory in the Chapel of St. George.

September 27

St. Akilina the Neo-Martyr
(1764)

The present-day invasion of Cyprus by the Turks, induced as a protective measure following clashes between the Greeks and Turks on the island, is nothing compared to the atrocities wreaked upon the hapless Greek nation for nearly five hundred years of Turkish tyranny. The defiled Churches, mutilated public buildings, and shattered masterpieces of ancient Greek art all bear mute testimony to the brutality of the Ottoman hordes who overran this time-honored peninsula in the most shameful chapter in history since the dawn of man.

The onslaught of the Moslem invaders was calculated to destroy not only their ideology in an extended orgy of murder, rape, and degradation, but to wipe out their faith in Jesus Christ, much as Communism seeks today to eliminate the worship of God. The Greek people offer living proof that Christianity is indestructible and that in keeping with their Christian teachings they can live in peace with their neighbors. But while Greek character as a whole withstood the oppression of centuries, there were cases in which the weak yielded to intimidation and threats.

One such man was the father of a girl whose name was Akilina, a man whose folly was for his daughter a two-edged sword that spelled death on the one hand, but immortality on the other. Having struck and killed a Turk in an argument that had nothing to do with religion, he was offered his freedom if he would disavow Christianity and become a Muslim. Furthermore, he had to promise that his daughter would also become a Muslim on attaining the age of 18. Her father agreed to this shabby agreement, much to the loathing of the Orthodox community which surreptitiously saw to it that his infant daughter would receive Christian training. By her eighteenth birthday, Akilina had grown not only into a creature of delicate beauty and high intelligence, but had also by then become a most devout Christian.

It was now time for the promise of her father to be fulfilled and she was summoned before the Turkish magistrate, who fully expected that as an obedient daughter she would honor her father's pledge. Impressed by her comeliness, he also contemplated the marriage of Akilina to one of his sons, a triumph over Christianity which would further damage the Orthodox image. To the surprise of the Turks and the solemn pride of the Greeks, not only did Akilina refuse to disavow Christ, but flatly declared that she would marry no one but a Christian. No amount of cajolery or threat could dissuade the girl from her firm stand for Christ. Consequently, she was ordered to be disgraced in public and to be tortured until she gave in to the Turkish demands.

What followed in this eighteenth century atrocity was reminiscent of the early years of the Church, when Christians were put to death with a callousness that beasts of the forest did not know. Akilina was lashed to a post in the public square, where a jeering Turkish mob gathered to mock her and spit in her face, among other things. One brute stepped out of the crowd and whipped the innocent girl until her clothes were in bloody shreds. He then stepped back to gloat and announced that he would be back the following day for more of the same unless she would change her mind during the night.

Some of her Greek friends managed to minister to the beaten girl, even promising it would not be held against her if she could no longer stand the punishment and gave in to her enemies. Even with the knowledge that her friends would still remain loyal whatever she chose to do, Akilina refused to deny Christ the next day and was again whipped unmercifully. This torture continued until the girl was a mass of bleeding welts and finally the Turks relented and released her. It was too late. While her friends carried her away from the scene of horror, she died. Akilina gave her life for Jesus Christ on 27 September 1764. She was eighteen years old.

Δ. Δukas

September 30

St. Gregory the Illuminator

There have been several saints of the Church named Gregory. Each has added to his name a title not so much to distinguish one from the other as to suggest what he is primarily remembered for. Although the title "Illuminator" distinguished the Gregory who is presently our subject, he was not so called just for the sake of avoiding confusion in names. He was called the "Illuminator" because he was a beacon of Christianity that brought the light of Jesus Christ to an entire nation.

Gregory the Illuminator was born into the royal family of Armenia during the reign of the Emperor Diocletian (284-314 A.D.). Fortunately for his native land, he was attracted to the new faith of Christianity, whose faint light he saw on the horizon when his countrymen were groping in spiritual darkness, lost in a welter of pagan ignorance and superstition. By birth he was destined to lead his people to what would have been the oblivion of paganism; by choice , however, he led his countrymen to the throne of Heaven through Jesus Christ by discarding the royal purple for the garb of the Christian priest.

His preparation for his future missionary work was completed under the pious Archbishop Leontios of Caesaria. The Archbishop must have wondered how the conversion of a nation steeped in pagan tradition could be brought about by a single priest, who had to pit the wisdom of Christianity against the ignorance of idolatry. But Gregory knew his people and went back to Armenia secure in the knowledge that they would ultimately come to Christ. The troubles that lay ahead would come from those in power, not from the common man whose parched soul needed to be watered by the love of the Savior.

It is common knowledge that Armenia became the first country to officially adopt Christianity as the religion of the realm. The events that brought this about were designed by the masterful and dedicated Gregory, whose unswerving loyalty to Christ brought distinction to his native land and spiritual laurels to himself. He built the first Armenian Church in the year 301 at a place called Etchmiadzin or "The Descent of the Only-Begotten." To this day the residence of the Patriarch of Armenia is still located there after 1600 years, except that it is now known as Yerevan in Soviet Armenia.

With each success in the development of Christianity, Gregory met mounting opposition from King Tiridates of Armenia, who thought it his duty to cling to paganism and to discredit Christianity. Failing to stem the Christian advance, the king ordered Gregory to be exiled. Thus he was exiled at Ararat, the place where Noah's Ark came to rest after the flood waters had receded. Little did the King know that the faith that was flooding his country would never evaporate. Expatriation soon proved not enough, and the King decided to heap all manner of indignities on the pious Gregory. He hoped to so weaken him physically and spiritually that his leadership would be rendered useless.

Accordingly Gregory was thrown into a pit, there to abide with the crawling creatures of the damp earth. Thus his enemies hoped that his spirit would be broken and that his cause would fail for lack of his guidance. It is estimated that Gregory lived in the ignominious pit for a period of 15 years. During this time he was kept alive with the help of Christians who dared to come to his assistance. His courage and steadfast loyalty to Christ served only to strengthen Christianity. Finally he was reluctantly released to complete his mission, which culminated in his conversion of the royal household itself and the conversion of Armenia to Christianity after centuries of spiritual stagnation.

Now under the Soviet yoke, Armenians pride themselves in their first unified acceptance of Christianity. No form of oppression can extinguish the light that was brought to them by Gregory the Illuminator, who died in 332 but lives today in the hearts of Christians everywhere.

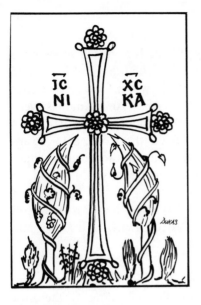

St. Ananias

The established doctrine of Jesus Christ as fully God and fully man easily survived a challenge in the 5th century. Although His Divine Nature sets him apart from mortals, He has had His counterparts as a man according to the Bible. Such a man was St. Ananias, one of the young men of the great Apostles of Christ, who fashioned his life after that of the Master. Although Ananias could measure up to Jesus only a fraction as a man, they had something in common. Ananias, like Jesus, was 33 years old at the time of his death.

The overwhelming majority of our saints are not mentioned in the Bible simply because they were men and women who were to become saints long after the New Testament had been written. Of those few, the Bible speaks of Ananias as being with St. Paul:

> And there was a certain disciple at Damascus named Ananias; and to him said the Lord in a vision, "Ananias." And Ananias said, "Behold, I am here Lord."
>
> And the Lord said unto him, 'Arise and go into the street which is called Straight, and inquire in the house of Judas for one called Saul, of Tarsus: for behold, he prayeth, and hath seen in a vision a man named Ananias coming in, and putting his hand on him, that he might receive his sight.'
>
> Then Ananias answered,"Lord, I have heard by many of this man, how much evil he hath done to thy saints at Jerusalem: and here he hath authority from the chief priests to bind all that call on thy name." But the Lord

said unto him, "Go thy way: for he is a chosen vessel unto me, to bear my name before the Gentiles, and kings and the children of Israel: for I will show him how great things he must suffer for my name's sake." And Ananias went his way, and entered into the house; and putting his hands on him, said, "Brother Saul, the Lord, even Jesus, that appeared unto thee in the way as thou camest, hath sent me, that thou mightest receive thy sight and be filled with the Holy Ghost."

And immediately there fell from his eye as it had been scales: and he received his sight forthwith, and arose, and was baptized. (Acts 9:10-19)

Thus, in one of the Bible's most stirring passages can be seen Christ's divine nature. It was the divine healing of the Lord that healed the blind man and it was the man Ananias through whom passed the divinity to perform the miracle. Ananias was chosen by Jesus to cure and baptize the sightless Saul, who became the greatest Apostle of them all in the service of Christ. Had the appointment of Ananias for this one act been his only blessing, he would have been assured a place among the greats of the Christian Faith.

But his work for Christ did not start nor did it end there. His life was one of piety, understanding, and brilliant scholarship. Historians tell us that St. Ananias carried Christ's message in a convincing manner in the Middle East and suffered martyrdom in the ancient city of Eleutheropolis. By command of the brutal anti-Christ ruler Lucian, St. Ananias was stoned to death. His memory is commemorated on October 1.

October 1

St. John (Koukouzelis)

The expression of emotion is best achieved through music, whose power ranges from the depths of lamentation to the heights of joy. A universal language was provided when the Lord gave man a singing voice, a talent with which many are gifted. Few have chosen to use this gift in the glorification of the Creator from whom it came. One who applied his golden voice almost exclusively to the glorification of God instead of earning fame and fortune was John Koukouzelis.

Born in the twelfth century in a province of Albania, John's exceptionally fine voice brought him to the Royal Academy of Music in Constantinople. There his natural talent was trained by teachers who marveled at the clarity and brilliance of his tone and brought him to the attention of the Emperor himself. He was summoned to the royal palace to perform for the Emperor. John's magnificent voice held a sophisticated audience in hushed reverence, and he was invited to share dinner with the royal household. When asked what was his favorite dish, John replied that he was partial to beans and peas, which brought on some good-natured laughter, and for which he was dubbed John Koukouzelis, which means beans and peas.

John was in much demand for the beauty of his voice, and with the Emperor as his patron, great things lay in store for him. He became a man of great importance and interest throughout the city because his artistry was one of the greatest of all time. The admiration of the music lovers who flocked to see him failed to bring him a sense of fulfillment; he felt there was something lacking in his purpose.

No doubt John had many hymns of faith in his repertoire,

and soon he found himself longing to get away from the crowds in order to find the solitude where he might draw nearer to God, rather than just singing about Him to the multitudes. After a chance meeting with an abbot of Mt. Athos who had been visiting Constantinople and who described the serenity to be found on the Holy Mountain, John made up his mind to leave the clamorous city. Fearing he would offend the Emperor who had so graciously sponsored him, he chose to slip out unnoticed and simply vanished, telling no one of his whereabouts.

He was received incognito at the monastery of the Great Lavra where the monks accepted him as a shepherd and where he assumed the duties of a novice. Unrecognized in his cloister, it was all he could do to refrain from joyfully singing, which would have revealed his identity. With his true identity a secret, he tended his flocks on the mountainside while the outside world wondered at his disappearance. At the Emperor's direction a search was underway for the voice that was no longer heard in sweet song, no longer lightening their burdens.

John meditated, prayed, herded his sheep, and drew even higher to God. One day while rounding up a stray sheep, he came upon a shrine of the Virgin Mary, to whom Mt. Athos is dedicated. Out of deep reverence he burst into a beautiful song of praise. By the time he had finished there wasn't a monk within hearing range who had not stopped to stand and listen. Soon he was singing the liturgies with such purity that the reputation he had sought to bury now revealed his true identity, for there was no other man who could sing like John.

The Emperor was pleased to have found his favorite vocalist, and instead of showing offense as John had feared, he said he would be delighted to have John return to even greater acclaim. Yet John preferred to remain at the Great Lavra. The abbot of the monastery journeyed to Constantinople to ask that John be permitted to remain a monk. Permission was granted, and after building a small chapel dedicated to the Archangels, John lived in piety and song until his death. His chapel has been the site of many miraculous workings of the Lord. He is remembered by the Church on October 1.

October 4

St. Peter of Capitolia

Out of respect for a highly revered saint in Christendom, the noble apostle of our Savior, St. Peter, parents in great numbers baptized their children after him. Despite the great popularity of the name it is surprising to discover that approximately forty of the Christian martyrs whose names we know carried the name of Peter. Of them, the first-century martyr, Peter of Capitolia, was unsurpassed in brilliance. In view of the brutality of his death, it is quite likely that none ever exceeded him in courage either.

History relates that the city of Capitolia, which is now known as Souvette, Syria, is the last resting place of the Biblical Job. The Christians who live there are rightfully proud that this honored ancient is one of them, at least geographically. They take perhaps greater pride in their native son who drew the attention of the civilized world to Capitolia by his service to Jesus Christ. For them the name of Peter of Capitolia is synonymous with Christian honor, dedication, and bravery.

The Apostle Peter preached in Syria for seven years, to be followed several years later by his namesake who did him honor in his pursuits of the propagation of the Christian faith. Married at an early age and the father of three children, Peter of Capitolia was encouraged to enter the priesthood. His success and fame as an educator and philosopher had put him in the public eye and he had culminated in his acceptance in the Church and his ultimate ordination as Archbishop of Bostra (Arabia). In this capacity, he displayed his prowess as a teacher and reverent servant of God. Dubbed "the teacher of the faithful," he converted countless thousands of Syrians to Christianity. In illuminating the spiritual darkness of his country with the light of Christianity, he inevitably made enemies. He was soon forced to account for his service to God and his disservice to the civil authority, whose rule was weakened by enlightenment of the people.

Summoned before the governor, this gallant defender of the faith strode into the hostile and pagan city of Damascus, whose governor had a reputation for unparalleled cruelty. Observing that his infamy had no obvious effect on Peter of Capitolia, the governor lost no time in holding the Archbishop up to scorn, ridicule, derision, and every manner of contempt. Questioned like a common criminal, the prelate's steadfast composure only stoked the fires of hatred that burned within the governor.

Peter of Capitolia was given his day in court, but a court in which the governor presided and held sway over a parade of witnesses whose testimony only bore out the great success of the accused man. In his own defense Peter would make the sign of the Cross when he mentioned the name of Jesus or the Blessed Virgin Mary. For this the governor ordered that the accused man's right hand be severed. When this did not stop Peter from praying, the order went out to mutilate him in a manner too horrible to relate. He was blinded, beheaded, even burned; what was left of his dismembered body was cast into the sea.

Christians in Syria today hold memorial seaside services for the gentle Peter of Capitolia, whose courage and faith has enriched the lives of all Christians.

October 9

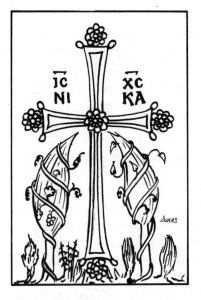

St. James the Less

Despite all effort to avoid it, the Church fathers painfully refer to a most venerated saint with an unflattering title to distinguish him from another with the same name. Nevertheless, St. James the Less is no less a man than the ninth apostle of the Lord. Church historians hasten to point out that St. James the Less is so designated solely because he was much shorter than his counterpart who is known as St. James the Greater. This paradox undoubtedly stems from a literal translation of the Greek language. However, many claim that St. James the Less was greater than St. James the Greater in perhaps all things but physical stature, which is man's measure, not God's.

St. James the Less was the son of Alpheos, while St. James the Greater was the son of Zebedee. Surprisingly little is known of James the Less, whose renown as an apostle is enough to place him among the greatest in Church history. That is not to say that he lived in obscurity. On the contrary, he was prominent in a time when the fires of Christianity were first ignited on earth. He was a brother to no other than St. Matthew, one of the four great Evangelists of the New Testament. His articulate oratory, his Christian zeal, and his complete dedication to the service of God and mankind were manifest throughout his lifetime when the cradle of Christianity was frail indeed.

The detailed events in his life which we now lack are accounted for perhaps by the way in which he lived. While successfully delivering the message of Christ to pagans in the Roman Empire, he was equally successful in eluding the Roman soldiers who were bent upon cornering him in some catacomb. Whenever St. James was on the brink of capture he would vanish, leaving the Emperor's nets to catch the wind. Leading them on a merry chase, he also led Church historians into a maze of appearances and disappearances that made a detailed biography of the man all but impossible. With his mission given to him by Jesus Himself, St. James lived and preached by his own wits in a pattern of behavior designed to perpetuate the name of Jesus Christ, not James the Less.

His most fiery sermons were saved for delivery in Palestine, where he preached with a zeal second to none and where his sincerity of purpose further added to the word of Christ. With the knowledge of his profound Faith, the Master allowed his beloved disciple to demonstrate the miraculous powers of Heaven. James served to perform many miracles in the name of Jesus, all the more perhaps because his prayers to the Lord were so fervent.

In the sixty-second year of our Lord, James died as did his Savior before him, by crucifixion at the hands of a generation that had followed those who crucified Christ. The day was October 9.

October 13

St. Florentios

Christian saints have all had in common the characteristics of faith and fortitude. But in this distinguished group of holy men and women there have been, as in other walks of life, those who remained in the ranks but marched to the beat of a different drummer. Any man who sets himself apart for any reason whatsoever may perhaps be called a controversial, provocative, or eccentric figure. There was a saint who was all of these things. The very mention of his name—Florentios—would set off a debate in his day. He was a crusading angel to his friends and anathema to his enemies, both of whom he had in great numbers.

St. Florentios lived during the Apostolic age of Christianity in the largely pagan but beautiful city of Thessalonike (Salonica), which had been so named for Thessalonike, the devoted sister of Alexander the Great. Florentios was an Orthodox Christian of unquestioned faith, but his *modus operandi* in delivering the work of Christ was somewhat unorthodox, primarily because he railed at paganism not only with boundless enthusiasm, but also with reckless abandon—and all this in the manner of a headless horseman.

His love for Christ was equalled by his unbridled loathing of paganism. At a time when society was predominantly pagan, Florentios' quixotic crusades naturally challenged the ruling political powers. Undaunted, he sneered at the gods of ancient Greece and publicly ridiculed those who would worship a graven image. His double-barreled attack was necessary, he reasoned, because he had to convince them both of the existence of one God and the appearance of the Son of God as their Savior. Florentios was equal to this task, but if he offended any sensibilities or trod on any toes, it mattered little as long as he could hammer home the truth.

Florentios would actually appear in the public square of Thessalonike, like an early-day demonstrator, and parade the length and breadth of the city's civic center, denouncing those who clung to the pagan gods. For this he was branded a rabble rouser by the pagans and a voice in the wilderness after John the Baptist by those who received his message. At this time he was appointed Bishop of Thessalonike by the small but durable band of Christians. While he may have shown the dignity of his office when necessary, he preferred to get into trenches where the real fighting was taking place.

Not content to preach the word of Christ in the cathedral where only Christians would hear him, Florentios courageously expounded the truths of the Christian faith in the courtyard of the pagan ruler. While delivering his oration, he was in effect delivering his own eulogy. The astounded court followers listened in disbelief as he dared to denounce the pagan gods as materials that would turn to dust. He urged them to turn to the one God that was spirit and was everlasting. His courage and faith stirred some minds to the truth, but he was to pay for it with his life.

Florentios was nailed to a cross and ordered to recant. With the remaining strength of his tormented body he proclaimed his faith in God and in Jesus Christ, His only-begotten Son. Still nailed to the cross, he was flung into a fiery pit and burned alive. In life he was controversial; in death he was immortalized.

October 14

St. Artemios

In the early years of the Byzantine Empire the ideological
concepts of a militaristic auto-
cracy stemmed from principles
that were both religious and
political in nature. Therefore
the posture of an outstanding
citizen of the day could be
that of a prelate statesman. At
a time when being a Christian
meant walking a thin line between life and death, politics were
so fused with religion that one could scarcely be separated from
the other. Even with the official establishment of Christianity as an accepted religion under Constantine the Great, the
menace to Christianity within as well as from outside the
Empire was formidable.

A defender of the faith of this era was St. Artemios, who as
ruler of Egypt could number himself among the highest social
figures of his time. After the death of Constantine, his successor and son Constantios carried on the warm relationship
with Artemios, who by then was firmly established as sovereign
of Egypt, a country whose decline Artemios had stemmed.
Artemios felt it his sacred duty to promote the welfare of his
subjects and to preserve and expand Christianity. His administrative excellence and religious ardor were the pride of the
people who for centuries had lived in the spiritual shadows of
the pyramids.

Artemios was accorded a high honor when he was appointed
by Constantios, himself a devout Christian, to seek out and
redeem the remains of two of our greatest saints. The body of
St. Andrew was entombed in Patras on the west coast of Greece,
and the body of St. Luke the Evangelist was interred in the city
of Thebes. It was no simple task to take these sacred relics
from the people of these two cities who cherished them. With

great diplomacy and conviction Artemios persuaded the respective communities to allow the translation of the relics of these two saints to the capital city of Constantinople.

Artemios, however, met his death at the hands of Julian the Apostate, one of the greatest enemies of Christianity. This avowed foe had renounced Christianity to embrace the pagan gods and had embarked on an assault upon Christianity without parallel for sheer savagery. Taking advantage of Constantios' preoccupation with the Persian war in the east, Julian's hordes, which were recruited from his native Gaul, invaded the Empire from the west. Constantios was equal to this treacherous act, but unfortunately he died of a fever before he could organize any substantial resistance to the invader.

With cunning subterfuge and all the evil guile at his command, Julian was able to form a Roman Byzantine Empire of which he declared himself Emperor. Now unchallenged, he launched a systematic persecution of the Christian people. It was in Syria that Christian blood began to flow in a campaign so inhuman it staggers the mind. But Julian had his eye on Egypt and for very personal reasons.

Julian had a brother who had been put to death in Egypt for treason. It did not matter whether his brother was innocent or guilty; it only mattered that he held Artemios responsible for his execution. Julian's brother was to be avenged in a manner as horrible as his evil mind could conceive. How this vengeance was carried out has been the subject of various accounts of the harshest possible tortures. It is certain, however, that Artemios met a cruelly violent death at the hands of Julian.

The holy remains of Artemios were removed to Constantinople and enshrined in the Church of St. John the Forerunner. His memory is celebrated on October 14.

October 17

St. Lazaros

Δ. Δukaς

Through the miracle of modern medicine, the life-sustaining machine can pump air into a lung, cause a heart to beat, or a kidney to function, but although it can sustain life, it cannot restore it. Restoration of life calls for a true miracle. Such a true miracle is recounted in the familiar story of how Jesus Christ recalled a man named Lazaros from a premature death by His divine grace. A spark of that divinity was transmitted to Lazaros in the process of his deliverance and instilled in him the grace with which he was to become a saint.

Such great emphasis is placed on the return of Lazaros from the dead that his prior life is practically ignored. His true life began after he had died, exactly four days after, since that was the period of time in which he had lain dead before Christ appeared at his tomb in Bethany. A true friend of the departed Lazaros, as well as of his grieving sisters Mary and Martha, Jesus stood before the tomb and commanded Lazaros to come forth, whereupon Lazaros stepped from oblivion into immortality. Thereafter he became a servant of the Lord in the early development of the new faith.

Following the death and Resurrection of the Savior, Lazaros undertook an apostolic mission which carried him to many corners of the Empire and ultimately to the island of Cyprus, where he settled after his ordination as Bishop of Kition. The Apostles of Christ encouraged him to stay on this island, and there he spent the final thirty years of his life, implanting Christianity with the firmness that was to sustain Cyprus centuries later through conquest, piracy, and subjugation. The association of Lazaros with Cyprus has been obscured by events on that strife-torn land, but evidence of his presence there is still extant after nearly two thousand years.

Christianity had taken a firm hold on the island when Lazaros died at the age of 58, this time not to be recalled by, but to join the Messiah who had summoned him many years before. He was buried in Cyprus and according to tradition there was inscribed after his name on his casket the words, "Tetraimeros, Friend of Jesus Christ." The word "tetraimeros" is translated the "fourth day," the day on which he was brought back from the grave. Moreover, he was honored in life as a friend of Jesus and was thus assured a place of honor in the kingdom of heaven.

Lazaros was entombed in a small chapel dedicated to his memory. More than 800 years later, Emperor Leo of Constantinople, himself a devout Christian, replaced the chapel which was threatened with ruin with a beautiful cathedral and monastery, a fitting tribute to the personal friend of Jesus. After a time, Leo decided that the proper resting place for St. Lazaros would be in the capital city of Constantinople. That project was probably frowned upon by the islanders who pridefully cherished the shrine of Lazaros, but in due course, they came to accept the plan to place Lazaros in a more hallowed setting. The remains of St. Lazaros were ceremoniously brought to the cultural center of Constantinople on 17 October 891.

A magnificent cathedral was erected in honor of St. Lazaros and his holy relics lie enshrined there in a bronze casket. The official dedication of the cathedral took place on 4 May 892. About the same time the remains of St. Mary Magdalene were also brought to Constantinople by the devout Emperor Leo. Thus the Emperor sought to honor these two friends of Jesus.

If a man can be measured by the kind of friends he has, then the measure of St. Lazaros cannot be drawn, because he had the friendship of Jesus Christ.

October 18

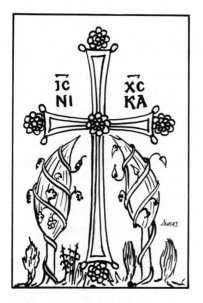

St. Luke the Evangelist

The awesome figure of St. Luke looms larger and larger out of both the New Testament and the pages of documented human history so that nearly two thousand years after his death his image has no less been diminished by time than that of the Nazarene, Jesus Christ, Whom he so nobly served. His fellow Apostle St. Paul called him the "glorious physician," but that was only one of the many talents which this magnificent man applied in a service to God. He was a man of such monumental proportion as to make him appear incredible. His many gifts were spiced with unswerving loyalty, prolific creativity, and matchless perfection.

Hailing from the ancient city of Antioch, Syria, Luke was a Roman whose early conversion to Christianity is evidenced by his membership in the Christian community of Antioch, prior to his emergence as an Apostle, after meeting Paul. He had by that time developed a remarkable command of the Greek language and employed its idiomatic expressiveness in his beautiful narrative form of recording history. He became the Church's most articulate historian and wrote with such sensitivity and clarity that his Gospel in the New Testament has been rightfully called the most beautiful book ever written.

Luke, a physician whose skills healed many of his suffering comrades, joined St. Paul on his second missionary journey, as recounted in the Acts of the Apostles. Their odyssey began in Troas, about A.D. 50, and took them to Phillipi, Rome, Caesarea, and ultimately to the Holy Land of Jerusalem. His prominence as a physician obscured his skills as an eloquent orator in the cause of Christ, but he was later to display a considerable talent as an artist whose icon of the Virgin

Mary he gave to the Mother of God herself and which is now the prized possession of the Patriarchate of Constantinople. Although his skill as a physician and talent as an artist may have by themselves given St. Luke a small place in history, it was his consummate gift as a writer that made him one of the greatest figures in all Christendom. Luke's contributions to the cause of Jesus Christ are beyond all measure, and his early influence on the Christian scene has enabled the Christian Church to rise to its ever increasing influence in human experience. One has only to read the Acts and his Gospel as well to realize the stature of this most holy man; however, it is reserved to the privileged few who can comprehend classical Greek that the sheer beauty of his language can be appreciated.

The praises of Luke as a writer may seem excessive, particularly since he is one of many authors represented in the New Testament, chief among whom are St. Matthew (the man), St. Mark (the lion), and St. John (the eagle). Among these, the fourth, St. Luke, suffers in comparison with the title 'St. Luke' (the calf). But out of the twenty-seven books comprising the New Testament, none shines with the brilliance of those composed by St. Luke. He is considered to have excelled beyond the others in expressiveness, historical method, narrative sensitivity, and idiomatic phrasing.

The patron saint of physicians and artists, St. Luke is surrounded by many legends and traditions that have not withstood the tests of time. The discounted accounts of his martyrdom must now give way to the actual facts of his life. It is known that he remained a bachelor all of his life, devoting himself to the utmost degree to the cause of Christ. When advancing years curbed his campaigning, he withdrew to write his memorable accounts and died in Thebes at the age of 84.

An appraisal of the contributions to Christianity by St. Luke cannot be measured by the number of words he wrote, the miles he traveled in missionary journeys, or the number of years he spent in exclusive dedication to the service of Jesus Christ. St. Luke, like so many who have given so much to all of us, is not to be appraised, only to be honored.

SAINT

GERASIMOS

Δ. Δukas

October 20

St. Gerasimos

On flights to Greece the jet pilots usually announce the approach to the Greek mainland by pointing out below on the sparkling Ionian waters the jewel-like island of Cephalonia. It is much more than a landmark. It is something more than its beautiful sister islands that surround the mainland. The very special reason is that its ground is the final resting place of St. Gerasimos, a saint whose body has miraculously remained in a state of preservation for nearly four hundred years.

Born in the rugged mainland of the Peloponnesos in the city of Trikkala in 1509, he set out on a peripatetic search for God that was a lifelong *tour de force*. His appetite for wisdom and piety was insatiable and he was never content to remain in one place for long, lest he grow too complacent in his religious practice. He had to crowd into his life all the holy places and all the holy men that he could possibly see. The result was that he made himself known to men of God in all the great centers of Christendom, including the isle of Zakynthos, Constantinople, the Holy Mountain, Chalcedon, Salonika, Damascus, and finally, in the sacred city of Jerusalem.

After some years in Jerusalem, Gerasimos was ordained a priest and thereafter tonsured a monk of the holy Church. During a twelve-year stay in the Holy Land, he established himself as a man of complete piety and rare proximity to God. His restless quest for total service to the Lord led him to visit the renowned monastery of St. Catherine in the Sinai Desert. He also visited a mountain retreat near the Jordan river called Sarantarion, the holy mountain where Jesus had remained for forty days and nights warding off the forces of evil. Likewise abiding there for forty days and nights, he returned to serve in the Patriarchate in Jerusalem.

While in charge of the Holy Church of the Resurrection in Jerusalem, the saintliness and wisdom of Gerasimos was made apparent in all his efforts. However, he still felt the need for even more spiritual refinement and led pilgrimages throughout the Holy Land, Egypt, Crete, and Zakynthos. At long last satisfied he had fulfilled all his spiritual obligations, he decided to settle in a place of his choice to make his stand for Christianity. He chose Cephalonia, to the dismay of so many other cultural and religious centers and to the great delight of the islanders.

A cave served as his headquarters, where people came for their spiritual needs. There he founded a pleasant nunnery which was named New Jerusalem and whose nuns were to render a great service in the name of the Lord. Gerasimos continued to teach and to inspire to the time of his death on 15 August 1579. He was buried in accordance with Orthodox tradition and, as was the custom of that day, he was exhumed after three years.

When the body of this venerated saint was exhumed, the world witnessed a miracle. His body was in a state of perfect preservation, as were his priestly robes. In addition to that there exuded from his casket an aroma like that of perfume. From all over Europe and the Middle East people made their way to look upon this holy man who lay there as though asleep. Encased in a glass casket at the nunnery on his beloved island, he lies in state to this day and is looked upon with sublime reverence by thousands of visitors each year.

October 23

St. James (Iakovos)

For a man whose kinship with Jesus Christ was so close that he has been referred to as the Brother of the Lord, when actually it is generally believed that he was a cousin to the Savior, surprisingly little is known to detail a full account of his life. The holy memory of his life was assured, if by nothing else than the simple fact that he was related to the Nazarene. But enough is known of the life of St. James to establish him as a saint on his own merits, as a man of God who, though not one of the original Apostles, equalled them in stature through his accomplishments in the early Christian Church.

It was through divine intervention that St. James came to acknowledge Jesus as the Son of God and through divine guidance that he came to be one of the founders of the Christian Church, as attested by the chapter of Corinthians in the New Testament of the Bible. In the dark days of paganism and spiritual ignorance, St. James espoused Christianity, the new religion, a crime which was tantamount to ostracism, in the least, and possibly the ultimate penalty of death. In the midst of this stark menace, he never wavered in his mission for Christ nor slackened his pace for the advancement of Christianity.

Dubbed St. James the Just for his piety and wisdom, St. James was a Nazarene, blessed with an endowment of righteousness. He was also equipped with a strength of character that was so imperative for the successful injection of the way of the Savior into the everyday life of the common, ignorant man, whose need for the knowledge of the Lord was critical. The many challenges to Christianity were met by St. James in masterful fashion and it is to him and the other early fathers of the Church that Christians owe a debt of gratitude for being able to rejoice in Jesus Christ.

After the Pentecost, St. James (Iakovos, to the Greeks) was entrusted with the sacred honor of converting the people of Jerusalem to Christianity, a mission in which he was eminently successful and which brought him a reputation that elevated him to the rank of Bishop of Jerusalem. Long a center of religious controversy, the city was to provide for St. James a platform for his mighty oratory, a platform which was, however, to be his scaffold for death. He was capable of stirring the passions of men, some of whom sought to destroy him but none of whom failed to admire and respect him.

It was as much out of respect for him, as well as envy, that an appeal was sent to him, the kinsman of the Lord, to answer the burning questions raised about the Messiah. In his answer the scribes and Pharisees had hoped they would find his condemnation, and the populace hoped it would end the doubts of some in their midst. He ascended to the rooftop of the temple in Jerusalem, flanked by those bent on destroying him and the threat his new Church represented. St. James might have equivocated or compromised in this perilous situation. He did neither. Refusing to disavow Christ, he openly declared his faith in Jesus and exhorted those below not to be intimidated into retaining old beliefs that would exclude them from the company of Christ.

The public demonstration of faith in Jesus Christ was more than his enemies could bear, and he was pushed off the rooftop, plunging to the courtyard below in a fall that should have killed him immediately. James survived, but only to be stoned to death. The date of his martyrdom is given as in the year A.D. 61, but it was not until late in the first century that true reverence was made to St. James, principally because few but the most scholarly in that period of great illiteracy came to know him through his eloquent epistle.

October 24

St. Sebastiane

Δ. Δυκας

The feminist movement somehow seems to be regarded as a modern day phenomnon stemming from an endeavor to respect the place of woman in what has previously been recognized as a man's world. If an activist in the feminist movement were to delve deep enough into the past, she would be pleasantly surprised to find that women played a major part in the growth of Christianity. The woman's role, in fact, goes back to the days of the Apostles, one of whom encouraged a young girl to take up the work of the Lord.

St. Paul, the man who wrote fourteen of the twenty-seven books of the New Testament, was responsible for the conversion and eventual sainthood of one of the first female followers of Christ. Her name was Sebastiane. In Marcianopolis in the province of Thrace, this girl who had never heard the name of Jesus Christ was among an assembly of people addressed by St. Paul.

The fame of St. Paul had preceded him and his oratory drew multitudes; consequently it was impossible for him to talk to each of his eager listeners in private audience following his lecture. A private audience with St. Paul was difficult to obtain and had to be arranged through Paul's inner circle responsible for his lecture tour. Having heard his words and being convinced of the truth and beauty of Jesus, the young Sebastiane, repentant of her sins and wishing to serve the Savior, was determined to meet St. Paul personally and make known to him her desire to serve.

Making her way through the crowd, she implored Paul's followers to take her to him. Acknowledging the Lord and reasserting her repentance, she was warmly embraced by St. Paul and was forthwith baptized.

St. Paul's travels through Greece are well known, particularly to those of the Orthodox faith, but less known is the fact that he had welcomed into his retinue the youthful Greek girl who had formerly been a pagan. The importance of her work in carrying the word of Christ throughout Greece soon increased. She earnestly helped bring the light of Christ's truth to those who were living in the spiritual darkness from which she had been drawn. By the time St. Paul left Greece she had become known throughout her native land as a woman of God.

During the reign of Domitian (A.D. 82), a time when it was dangerous to be a Christian in secret, let alone avow it publicly— the undeniable evidence of her closeness to God was manifested by her good works and her miracles performed in the Lord's name. A spiritual force to be reckoned with, she worked tirelessly for God, heedless of the warnings that her life was now in real jeopardy. The governor, Sergios, an avowed enemy of Christianity who totally disregarded her sex, dispatched her to a dungeon cell, thereafter to be put to torture for her crime against the state.

Encouraged by a vision of St. Paul, she was undaunted as she was led to the brink of a fiery pit. Just as she was tossed into the conflagration a torrent poured from the heavens and extinquished the blaze and Sebastiane emerged completely unharmed. This so frightened Sergios that he wanted no more of her and ordered her returned to her native Heracleia in Thrace. There the power of the Lord again was evidenced when two lions to whom she was tossed behaved as kittens with her. Finally, led from the city, she was beheaded. It was as though the Lord had spared her from a lingering death to that of swift martyrdom. She died on 23 October 83.

October 29

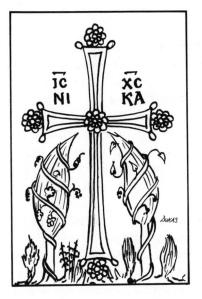

St. Anastasia of Rome

If it is easier for a camel to pass through the eye of a needle than for a rich man to enter the kingdom of Heaven, then it should have been virtually impossible for the beautiful and glamorous Anastasia to enter the service of Christ. The attributes that make for living a life of ease in the grand style are obstacles to be surmounted if one prefers to lead a life of hard work in a simple manner for the glory of God. To her everlasting credit, Anastasia, who was born with every advantage, willingly surrendered the flower-strewn path of her noble birth to walk down the perilously rock-strewn path of Christianity.

Anastasia was born into one of Rome's most celebrated families in the third century. Reared in the comfortable circumstances of nobility, knowing nothing of poverty or deprivation, she was endowed with a rare beauty of face and form which became the envy of many women of her station. At a time when most young women take full advantage of their position and charm, she made a dramatic turn to Christ with the full awareness that her commitment would cost her more than the material wealth she abandoned.

She was scarcely nineteen years old when the spirit of Christianity flourished within her and revealed a beauty of soul which exceeded her beauty of face. It is ironic that her breathtaking physical beauty would prove to be her undoing, for she died an early death primarily because of envious females. Her new Christian faith was all that mattered to Anastasia, and she sought the advice of her Christian friends as to how she could best serve the Lord. Fearing for her safety because she had offended the ruling class that frowned on Christianity, they suggested she leave the area.

Anastasia had no desire to leave the country of her birth. Thus, as an alternative she chose the life of an ascetic within eremitic confines not too far removed from Rome. She directed her educated and highly trained mind to the cause of Christ. Her reputation for piety and sacrifice was such that soon others were disowning their social order to follow her example. This made her all the more unpopular in the higher Roman circles, particularly among the pagan women who not only envied her beauty, but came to hate her for her successful transition.

Charges of treason were brought against Anastasia, and she was summoned before the provincial governor, Probius. Marvelling at her beauty, he was nevertheless annoyed by her refusal to embrace the pagan gods. She remained steadfast in her allegiance to Christ, all the while knowing the governor's annoyance would soon turn to vengeful wrath, which it indeed did. Because of her great beauty, however, he decided to let his decadent court have some sport, and Anastasia was forced to parade naked before a jeering audience that included the palace guard.

Soon tiring of this, the governor turned her over to the brutes who specialized in tormenting victims of the state's wrath. She was ultimately beheaded on 29 October 258 and her remains were left along the roadside near Rome. She lay there for weeks in a state of preservation that was such that no insect or bird sought to prey on her flesh. At length a group of Roman Christians snatched the once beautiful Anastasia and gave her a Christian burial.

November 1

SS. Cosmas and Damian

Christianity flourished in antiquity in the face of seemingly insurmountable odds. In defiance of odds of a different kind, the odds of chance, a pair of physician brothers came into the service of Christ. Less than five hundred years later they were followed by two different sets of brothers of identical name and purpose in the service of the Lord. The result is that all six have become saints of the Church. Evidence of divine purpose in this succession of saints demonstrates that the precise science of mathematical probabilites—chance—has a hand in the spiritual affairs of mankind.

The original pair of brothers were born Cosmas and Damian during the early years of the Christian Church. They were raised in comfortable circumstances in a comparatively wealthy family which saw to their thorough training of mind and body in Asia Minor. Endowed with keen intellect, the brothers became inseparable in common pursuit of the science of medicine. Both firmly believed that "of the most high cometh healing" and were aided in their work by religious devotion. As students they vowed to supply their medical skill without charge to a suffering Christian community and thereby prince and pauper alike were to feel the balm of their healing art.

Dubbed the "unmercenaries" for their refusal to accept money for their services, they also came to be acknowledged as miracle workers for the remarkable cures they were able to effect. Their parents' estate had provided for their well being, but it was to last them only through strict austerity; they could not afford any of the comforts which could have been theirs if they had chosen to charge their patients for their services.

As time went on, the brothers' love of the Savior became more and more evident, subordinating even their great devotion to medical science. The word miracle had a literal meaning for their great work as physicians, for only through the power of the Lord could they have brought about such healing of those afflicted with serious and often terminal illnesses.

Such was the veneration in which the brothers were held in their own lifetime that they remained unchallenged by even the most avowed pagan enemies of Christianity. They carried on their work for God and man all the years of their lives, which were full, and they died peacefully of natural causes quite unlike the saints who were to die for Christ in agony.

It is not uncommon for parents to name children for someone dear to them or for some great figure in the Church. In keeping with this tradition, a pair of brothers of a wealthy Roman family were named Cosmas and Damian in honor of the master physicians and saints of Asia Minor. The lives of this second pair of saints with identical names paralleled those of the original pair. They emulated their predecessors in every detail and were also venerated in their own lifetime as miracle-working physicians and men of God. The similarity ends, however, with the manner of their death, because the hostile Romans did not allow them to lead their lives to the fullest in the service of God, and they suffered martyrdom at the hands of their enemies.

A third pair of physician saints appeared in ancient Arabia, and remarkably enough they were named Cosmas and Damian. The lives of this third pair are not detailed in any extant accounts of the saints, but it is known that they also served in the manner of the original saints and that they were martyred in the manner of the second pair. The original saints Cosmas and Damian are honored on the feast day of Nov. 1; the second pair of saints on July 1, and the third pair on October 17.

November 8

St. Simeon the Translator

In the ninth century a man's concern for a biographical record of the saints of the Church up to his day led to a monumental work of scholarship and research to the degree that he himself was rewarded with sainthood. This most literate luminary of his time was St. Simeon the translator, so named for his in depth study of the Church and its saints, a prodigious labor of love which entailed a great deal more than a mere translation.

Endowed with a tremendous intellect, St. Simeon rose to prominence as chief magistrate and advisor to Emperor Leo the Wise, who was indeed wise enough to heed the counsel of his magistrate. The talents of Simeon included those of tact and diplomacy, which were to stand the ninth century Byzantine Empire in good stead, for those were times when an astute diplomat could avoid bloodshed at the hands of the hostile hordes outside the civilized empire, particularly those of the Middle East.

The non-Christian Arab tribes with their militaristic chieftains posed a constant threat to the eastern flank of the Empire. At this time the island of Crete, so near the Asian coast, was being ravaged by Arabs swooping upon islanders in vicious forays. Leo the Wise saw the need for diplomatic intervention in lieu of military action and called upon Simeon.

Simeon brought about a peaceful solution to the problem largely through his consummate skill as a diplomat. He returned in triumph to Constantinople to be hailed as the most able statesman of his day. Leo the Wise was prepared to lavish upon Simeon the highest laurels the Empire could bestow, as well as generous gifts and estates. Simeon, however, asked the monarch that he be granted one request for which he had longed — to be allowed to withdraw from public life for one of meditation and prayer. A reluctant Leo the Wise granted Simeon his wish, whereupon Simeon launched a career in scholarly research unparalleled in the history of the Church.

Simeon, a devout Christian from birth, had nurtured a desire for many years to seek out all the facts about the saints and martyrs of the Church whom he had admired from a distance while a layman in the service of the Emperor. Through an exhaustive combination of research and scholarship, which he funded himself from whatever wealth he had accumulated, he compiled his magnificent "Lives of the Saints" which has taken its place as part of our religious heritage.

Sparing no effort or expense, Simeon gathered a great abundance of material, writings in every form and in every language from every part of the Empire and beyond. He sifted through documents, recorded data, civil and Church records and various accounts which might shed some light on the life and times of the great figures of ecclesiastical history. After long research, he put his remarkable book into the Greek language. The translation from many tongues into the Greek was perhaps the least of his labor, but nonetheless this earned him the title of Simeon the Translator.

While literature was undeniably his forte, his talent in music as well was such that many of the hymns he composed remain in the Orthodox Church services. This prolific servant of God saw the fulfillment of his life's ambition and accepted with humility the deep respect of Christianity to the end of his well-numbered years.

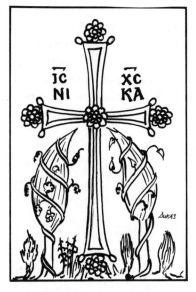

St. Nektarios,
the Modern Saint (1920)

The title of saint is not easily come by in any age, but it is even more difficult in the twentieth century, when being a Christian presents none of the hazards of declaring faith in Jesus Christ which the early Christians met with such heroism, thereby earning sainthood. Neverthless, there was a man in this century whose spiritual light shone with such brilliance that he took his place alongside the saints, whose ranks have closed even tighter with the passing of the centuries. In an age when the only fear a Christian need have was the fear of a fellow Christian, a man named Nektarios rose above the complacency of the Christian community into which he was born to attain the stature of a most holy man among most holy men.

Nothing out of the ordinary concerning his birth or formative years carried any portent of the spiritual giant Nektarios was destined to become. He was born in Selybria, Thrace, now a part of modern Turkey, in October of 1846. He was an average figure in a prosaic setting—and possessed a very limited degree of literacy—until he was fourteen, when he went to seek work in Constantinople. In that ancient capital, however, he evidently found himself and by the time he was 21 he was an accomplished scholar and a most devout Christian. Conversant in the classics and immersed in religious learning, he entered a monastery on the island of Chios. Later he entered the service of Patriarch Sophronios of Alexandria, Egypt, who gave him a scholarship to study theology at the University of Athens. After his theological studies he was ordained a priest to serve in Cairo, Egypt, where his success earned him elevation to the episcopate. The forces of envy, however, followed Nektarios with each success, and he soon found himself assailed by enemies in his very own Christian community. When so much pressure was brought to bear on Patriarch Sophronios,

Nektarios was stripped of his authority and duty. This grievous injustice spurred him to greater achievements in Athens where his great wisdom was reasserted. It was not long before his popularity as preacher and theologian brought countless invitations to preach in the many churches of the ancient capital and led to his appointment as dean of a theological school in 1894.

This appointment could have been an oasis for a less determined clergyman, but for Nektarios it was the launching pad for meteoric achievements in the service of Jesus of Nazereth. Among other things, he established a convent for nuns—a lovely cloister named in honor of the Holy Trinity—on a small island just off the coast of Piraeus known as Aegina. When he reached the age of retirement, he left behind the ease and comfort of the city to go to a small retreat he had seen on the tiny island.

A man who walked with God, Nektarios was sought out on his island retreat by many of the faithful and his kindness and piety were seen by the countless pilgrims he welcomed. A second chapel within the convent walls was erected and it was in this chapel that Nektarios was buried when he died on 9 November 1920. But the story of Nektarios does not end with his death. People continued to travel to the island to pray at what was then the shrine of a renowned bishop, but not yet a saint. With reports of miraculous cures at his grave, the stream of pilgrims continued and the island teemed with those who sought a closeness to God by proximity to the late bishop. The pilgrimages to the convent of the Holy Trinity continued through the years and culminated in 1961 when a proclamation of the Patriarchate declared sainthood for Nektarios, forty-one years after his death.

Considered as the patron saint of people stricken with cancer, heart trouble, arthritis and epilepsy, among other illnesses, Saint Nektarios reposes on his tiny island, venerated by Orthodox Christians everywhere. Many of the elderly faithful were privleged to have seen him and now glory in telling their children or grandchildren how they were in the company of a man who is now a Saint of God.

The veneration of St. Nektarios is quite widespread in America and is increasing daily. More and more churches now display his icon, which can also be found in thousands of homes of Orthodox Christians.

St. John Chrysostom

The legion of saints of the Church is comprised of men of extraordinary ability whose talents may have been dissimilar but many of whom seem to have shared a common genius for oratory. Yet out of this vast assembly of eloquent speakers whose reputation might have rested on their gift of expression alone, the one for whom the title 'Chrysostom,' or 'golden-mouthed,' was reserved was John of Antioch, known as St. John Chrysostom, a great distinction in view of the qualifications of so many others.

Endeared as one of the four great doctors of the Church, St. John Chrysostom was born in 347 in Antioch, Syria and was prepared for a career in law under the renowned Libanius, who marveled at his pupil's eloquence and foresaw a brilliant career for his pupil as statesman and lawgiver. But John decided, after he had been baptized at the age of 23, to abandon the law in favor of service to the Savior. He entered a monastery which served to school him in preparation for his ordination as a priest in A.D. 386. From the pulpit there emerged John, a preacher whose oratorical excellence gained him a reputation throughout the Christian world, a recognition which spurred him to even greater expression that found favor with everyone but the Empress Eudoxia, whom he saw fit to criticize in some of his sermons.

When St. John was forty-nine years old his immense popularity earned him election to the Patriarchate of Constantinople, a prestigious post from which he launched a crusade against excessiveness and extreme wealth which the Empress construed as a personal affront to her and her royal court. This also gave rise to sinister forces that envied him his tremendous influence. His enemies found an instrument for his indictment when they discovered that he had harbored some pious monks who had been excommunicated by his archrival Theophilos, Bishop of Alexandria, who falsely accused John of treason and surreptitiously plotted his exile.

When it was discovered that the great St. John had been exiled by the puppets of the state, there arose such a clamor of protest, promising a real threat of civil disobedience, that not even the royal court dared to confront the angry multitudes and St. John was restored to his post. At about this time he put a stop to a practice which was offensive to him, although none of his predecessors outwardly considered it disrespectful; this practice was applauding in Church, which would be considered extremely vulgar today, and the absence of which has added to the solemnity of Church services.

St. John delivered a sermon in which he deplored the adulation of a frenzied crowd at the unveiling of a public statue of the Empress Eudoxia. His sermon was grossly exaggerated by his enemies, and by the time it reached the ears of the Empress it resulted in his permanent exile from his beloved city of Constantinople. The humiliation of banishment did not deter the gallant, golden-mouthed St. John, who continued to communicate with the Church and wrote his precious prose until he died in the lonely reaches of Pontus in 407.

The treasure of treatises and letters which St. John left behind included the moving sermon that is heard at Easter Sunday services. The loss of his sermons which were not set down on paper is incalculable. Nevertheless, the immense store of his extant literature reveals his insight, straightforwardness, and rhetorical splendor, and commands a position of the greatest respect and influence in Christian thought, rivaling that of other Fathers of the Church. His liturgy, which we respectfuly chant on Sundays, is a living testimony of his greatness.

The slight, five-foot St. John stood tall in his defiance of state authority, bowing only to God and never yielding the high principles of Christianity to expediency or personal welfare. In the words of his pupil, Cassia of Marseilles, "It would be a great thing to attain his stature, but it would be difficult. Nevertheless, a following of him is lovely and magnificent."

November 14

St. Philip, the Apostle

St. Philip was born in a remote corner of the Holy Land, in a tiny village named Bethsaida. This village is also the birthplace of St. Peter and St. Andrew as well. Philip, like the other apostles of Christ, was assigned an area to which he would preach the word of Christ by the drawing of lots. To him fell the uninviting western area of the continent of Asia, or Asia Minor as it has been called. He assumed this responsibility with a confidence and humility born of the blessings of the Lord. He was more than ably assisted in this holy work not only by his devout sister Miriam, but by the Apostle Bartholomew as well. Their efforts were assured success when the Lord chose to make St. Philip an instrument of miraculous powers.

He traversed the length and breadth of Asia Minor tirelessly preaching and doing good work. He then returned for a time to Greece where, like St. Paul before him, he preached before throngs of Greeks in Athens. Then he brought countless numbers of Hellenes into the Christian fold with the assistance of Bartholomew and Miriam.

St. Philip's return to Asia was hastened by reports of a strange Phrygian cult which had been introduced to the superstitious and illiterate populace and which was in direct conflict wih Christian doctrine and practice. A snake of awesome size was being worshipped as a god, but with greater reverence than a whole herd of sacred cows, as in India. The colossal viper was said to be invincible, a notion which vanished when St. Philip strode up to the creature and placed his hand on it causing it to perish on the spot. This display brought the populace back to its senses and by thousands the Phrygians were baptized into Christianity.

To say that this caused the pagan fanatics considerable consternation would be quite an understatement. They became enraged and set their minds on destroying the holy trio of Philip, Bartholomew, and Miriam. Tried and condemned, the servants of God were sentenced to be crucified. The death sentence was carried out with dispatch and the holy three were nailed to wooden crosses. No sooner had this been done than the sky darkened and the earth trembled violently from a rumbling earthquake. This phenomenon struck terror into the hearts of those responsible, who immediately sought to appease the wrath of God by taking the intended victims down from their crosses.

Miriam and Bartholomew survived, but as though he had willed his own demise so that his death might be on the heads of his enemies, St. Philip did not. His dying gaze rendered the throng powerless and he bled to death on November 14 with his last breath praising the Lord.

November 14

St. Gregory Palamas
(Second Sunday of Lent)

The magnificent monastic cloister of Mount Athos in Greece first became the dwelling place of hermits before A.D. 850. Later, in 963, it was officially established by Athanasios of Trebizond with the help of his friend and patron Nicephoros II Phocas. Subsequently, a spiritual community of several monasteries developed, of which today there are twenty. Mount Athos was plundered after a Fourth Crusade in 1204 and was again ravaged by the Catalans in 1307-1309, leaving it for years in near ruin. It declined to near extinction until its revival by a group of monks, notable among whom was St. Gregory Palamas. It survival was assured by this pious monk who was later to become an archbishop and who found eternity in his service to the Lord.

Gregory Palamas was of noble parentage and was raised in the splendor of the royal palace of Constantinople. In spite of the comforts and glory of his surroundings, he had a yearning to work for Christ. He fulfilled this desire at an early age when he abandoned the life of ease in Constantinople in exchange for the life of an ascetic at a monastery of Mount Athos. He found there not only the means to spiritual attainment, but also a challenge to restore this monastic haven to the influential spiritual center it had once been. He therefore prevailed upon Andronicos II to have this spiritual bastion placed under the jurisdiction of the Patriarch of Constantinople.

This close association of Mt. Athos with the Patriarchate was cemented by St. Gregory's support of the doctrine of hesychasm, the type of Eastern Christian monastic life whose purpose is to achieve divine quietness (hesychia) through the contemplation of God in uninterrupted prayer. This concept, offered by St. John of the Ladder (Climacos) and refined by St. Nicephoros the Hesychast, was defended by Gregory Palamas. According to St. Gregory and the hesychasts, the human body is sanctified by the sacraments and participates through the senses in the prayer offerings. Although the Patriarch supported the beliefs of the hesychasts, their views were challenged by others. A great controversy ensued. The net result was that councils were convened and the teachings of Gregory Palamas were affirmed by the Church and were officially recognized.

The restoration of the monasteries was the cherished goal of Gregory, who looked upon the once imposing spiritual fortress with deep concern but with an even deeper determination to rekindle this beacon of Christianity into an eternal flame. With the assistance of the Patriarch he recruited lay workmen to rebuild the monasteries and to construct new ones for the ever-increasing number of monks. Thus, Gregory's vision of a stronghold where prayer and meditation would strengthen the cause of Christianity throughout the world became a reality.

November 16

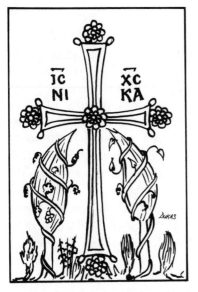

St. Matthew the Evangelist

Any reference to the Apostle St. Matthew, author of the first book of the New Testament, is made with such solemnity and reverence that speaking of him as a man seems almost sacrilegious, so close to the divine is he considered. But when Jesus came upon Matthew, he was a man who could scarcely be viewed with little but contempt by the human eye; the divine sight of Christ, however, saw in this man which He beckoned to His service that spark of greatness invisible to the rest of the world. It is doubtful that Matthew himself was aware of what lay dormant in him that was to place him in the forefront of Christianity.

Matthew was a native of Cana, the scene of the wedding feast at which Jesus performed his first miracle of changing the water to wine. He became a tax collector for the Roman government, a position that has endeared no one to the taxpayer at any time in history, but which in the time of Christ, when the populace was taxed to excess, was deemed second in unpopularity only to the executioner. Jesus was traveling on the Mediterranean Damascus road when he came upon Matthew who was stationed there in his inglorious pursuit. Standing at a lake near the city of Capernaum, Matthew's gaze met the Lord's and Jesus spoke to him, uttering only two words: "Follow me."

Thus, in most unceremonious fashion did the divinity of Christ assert itself and an overwhelmed Matthew took up the cause of Christ without any reply. He was no doubt so overcome with emotion at the majestic power of Jesus that he could not speak, but the communication between them was clear and Matthew felt a resurgence of the spirit within him and came to know the tranquility that emanates from God.

The service of St. Matthew is familiar to all who call themselves Christian. His close association with Jesus tends to obscure the man who shed the ignominious role of tax collector to become the most intellectual of the twelve Apostles chosen by the Lord. The awesome task of carrying the word of Christ to a people oppressed for centuries and suspicious of any newcomer was assumed by St. Matthew with a determination that could not be denied. If the fifteenth century civilization could laugh at Columbus who said the world was round, what did they say to Matthew fifteen hundred years earlier when he declared that Jesus was the Son of God. In simple terms, it wasn't easy. Matthew says it in Chapter 10:16 when he quotes Jesus as saying to his disciples: "Behold, I send you as sheep in the midst of wolves."

After the crucifixion of Christ and His Resurrection, the inspiration of the Master was reaffirmed with renewed vigor at Pentecost when all the Apostles were enlightened by the Holy Spirit. Christianity owes its existence to the indomitable will and courage of the Apostles, who surmounted great obstacles of disbelief, superstition, distrust and open hostility in spreading the gospel. There was no mass media, only the word of mouth and the weary foot travel from village to village. Christianity is the greatest single achievement in the history of mankind and to St. Matthew and his ten comrades goes the credit for having successfully spread the worship of Jesus Christ.

Matthew preached the Gospel for many years after the death of Christ, travelling throughout the Holy Land and finally meeting a martyr's death at the hands of pagans in Ethiopia. His final verse is his epitaph. "Teaching them to observe all things whatsoever I have commanded you: and, lo, I am with you always, even unto the end of the world. Amen." The feast day of St. Matthew is observed on November 16.

November 25

St. Katherine

Man's important invention, the wheel, has come to symbolize every form of advancement and often we refer to the wheels of progress or the wheel of fortune or fate. For a martyred saint of Egypt in the fourth century, however, the wheel became the symbol of death as stark as the guillotine of France. When St. Katherine died in agony on a spiked wheel —devised to make her death a protracted process of pain—her lifelong radiance as a brilliant Christian continued to glow and is still manifest in the shrines that have been erected in her memory.

Lacking the forms of communication that were to develop mankind's intellectual and spiritual interests, the society of the early centuries relied on the public forum for this sole source of information and stimulation of thought. This accounts for the great popularity of this form of expression which brought to the public's attention great figures of the time who might otherwise have gone unnoticed. Into this atmosphere of public discourse came one of the brightest minds of Christianity, that of a mere girl named Katherine, who early in life displayed the wisdom of ages and championed the cause of Christianity with an eloquence unsurpassed by her male counterparts.

The presence in the city of Alexandria, Egypt, of the pious and astute Katherine was unknown until she made her debut at the age of eighteen in the public forum in defense of the Christian faith. The defenders of Christianity had fared badly in the public debates, principally because the most powerful orators of the day espoused the pagan beliefs and had little difficulty in making sport of Jesus, the Son of God, whose followers were long on faith but short in numbers. But the pagan philosophers were a Goliath against the David who appeared in the form of a wisp of a girl called Katherine.

With the quiet dignity that stemmed from her noble birth, the beautiful Katherine impressed the forum audience from the moment she strode forth to speak. When she had parried every pagan thrust in a torrent of rhetoric that routed her opponents, the public was virtually spellbound. In the process of throwing the haughty pagan thinkers into a state of confusion, she captured the hearts of the listeners. Those who had welcomed her to the forum hoping that she would be driven from it in derision were themselves driven in angered frustration to seek out a means of silencing this frail creature whose Christian sagacity was winning converts as fast as they could assemble.

An appeal was made by Katherine's enemies to the Emperor Maxentius, who authorized the tyrant Maximus Daza (A.D. 36) to mete out whatever punishment deemed necessary for the crimes against the state enumerated by sycophants of the pagan ruler. Her friends looked on helplessly as the devout woman who had labored for Christ was led away to face the stern justice handed down to the so-called enemies of the state. The courageous Katherine denied the customary offer of clemency in exchange for a disavowal of the Savior. They therefore decided that she be put to death in a manner so cruel as to discourage any other Christian, man or woman, from exposing himself to the wrath of pagan justice.

The example they sought to make of Katherine, fiendish as it was, turned instead into an example of the superhuman courage of the Christian martyr, the kind of Christian who could endure excruciating pain in the name of Jesus Christ. The redoutable girl was placed on a wheel of spikes which was revolved; the centrifugal force of the wheel produced an inhuman torture on the body until at last death came as an escape from the harsh world of the flesh to the arms of the Savior. The lovely Katherine died on 25 November 311 and eventually her remains were brought to the monastery of Mt. Sinai which bears her name and where thousands of pilgrims annually pay homage to one of the sweetest Christians in history. An icon of St. Katherine invariably depicts her impaled upon the wheel on which she rolled to Heaven.

SAINT MΕRCURIOS

Δ.Δυκας
1776

St. Mercurios

In the days of antiquity, particularly in the third century, military men were held in the highest esteem and occupied the top strata of the many-layered social structure of the mighty Roman Empire. It was to the military that the Emperor looked for their support, and it was the military conquests that added wealth and glory to the Empire. Mercurios was a Roman officer in the best tradition of military service. Intrepid on the field, a bold and efficient leader of men in the campaigns, he was sought after in the social circles of Rome not only because of his military prowess, but also because he was a splendid figure in uniform, handsome of feature, and charming of wit.

Mercurios carried out his duties in exemplary manner and was the delight of the high command. He was also the best swordsman in his regiment; in battle he was a tactician that assured victory in every encounter with the enemy. His warlike stance belied the Christian spirit within him because despite his vocation he was a true believer in Jesus Christ, something which he never revealed to those about him. His reasons were twofold. In the first place Christianity was frowned upon as the philosophy of the weak and secondly, not only his position but his life depended on keeping his Christian faith a secret.

According to a biographer, Mercurios had a vision on the eve of a great battle in which an angel of the Lord foretold that he would not only be victorious, but that he would also slay King Regas, whose army the Romans were facing. On the day of the battle, Mercurios and his cohorts successfully fought off the hordes of barbarians and at the height of the conflict, Mercurios found himself facing King Regas, whom he dispatched with a stroke of his sword. Their king fallen, the tattered remains of the foe fled to the hills. Thereafter Mercurios was received in triumph by the Emperor Decius who forthwith appointed him a general. He was only twenty-five years old when he received that high military appointment and was soon swept into a swirl of pomp in his honor throughout the city. If all the world loves a hero, then the Romans positively adored them and Mercurios was so preoccupied with his new life of glamor and tribute that he neglected to take part in the services of the Church. The same angel who had visited him on the eve of battle reappeared and admonished him for forsaking the Church. With abject repentance, he assured the angel he would resume his active participation in Christian worship.

A young officer of Mercurios' regiment, jealous of his general and ever wary for some way in which to discredit him, began to notice that at any feast honoring the Roman gods, Mercurios was conspicuous by his absence. One evening the young officer surreptitiously followed Mercurios and discovered that he was worshipping in secret in the Church of Christ. He could hardly wait to bring the news to Emperor Decius, who immediately registered disbelief that a Roman general would turn Christian.

When Mercurios was brought to face the unhappy Decius, he refused to deny he was a Christian. When informed that the whole thing would be forgotten if he displayed his allegiance by praying to the gods, Mercurios declared he would pray only to God and only in the name of Jesus Christ. This left the Emperor no alternative and he ordered that Mercurios be executed in a manner prescribed for Christians. He died for Christ on November 25.

As a postscript to the story of Mercurios, history relates that Decius and his successor came to a violent end and that a century later, according to St. Basil, Mercurios was sent by the Lord to punish Julian the Apostate, who had denied Christ and was therefore killed in a battle as punishment for having sent so many Christians to their death while he reigned.

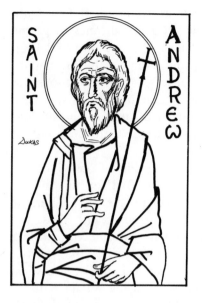

November 30

St. Andrew

It is comforting to those who are bringing up the rear in the Christian march to Heaven to hear the words: "The first shall be last and the last shall be first." Nevertheless, just as the first president of the United States is more revered than any who have succeeded him, their credentials notwithstanding, the first to be called by Jesus Christ into His service commands a reverence a degree greater than those who have followed for the simple reason that he was the first man beckoned by the Son of God. The high honor of being so chosen went to a man named Andrew, called Proklitos or 'first-called,' who went on to prove himself worthy of distinction in his eminently successful apostolic missions.

Andrew, like his brother Peter, was a fisherman, a toiler with net and boat recognized in the Psalms of the Old Testament as one of those "who go down to the sea in ships, that do business in great waters; these see the works of the Lord and His wonders in the deep." His love of the sea stemmed from his love of the Creator who made it, and the perils of the sea which he challenged daily forged the character with which he boldly assailed the seas of ignorance and paganism in the sacred trust that had been placed in his keeping.

Andrew, who lived in the Holy Land in the ancient city of Bethsaida, accepted Christ with all his heart and after an indoctrination with St. John the Baptist went forth to become one of the greatest missionaries in all history. When the Apostles drew lots to determine their sphere of labor for the Savior, Andrew exulted in his mission to preach in Asia Minor, part of Greece, and an area along the coast of the Black Sea, including its gateway, the city now known as Istanbul, or Constantinople. Wherever Andrew went he attracted throngs of people who thirsted for a spiritual knowledge. His message of deliverance was so eloquently convincing, even to hostile minds, that he is credited with having converted countless thousands to Christianity in a day when mass media did not exist. As an Apostle, his only tools were his power of oratory and his love for Jesus, and his only press agent was the word of mouth of those privileged to hear his homilies.

Andrew came to Jerusalem for the First Council of the Apostles, about A.D. 50, another historic first for him and the other Apostles, some of whom he had not yet met. There he rejoiced in joining the great St. Paul together with those but for whom Christianity might never have become the glorious human experience it is today. Out of this Council the Apostles went forth with renewed vigor to establish the ecclesiastical system. Andrew alone is credited with having set up parishes throughout Asia Minor, in Pontus, Bithynis, Thrace, Macedonia, Greece, Scythia (Russia, where he is still regarded as patron saint) and in the capital city of Byzantium.

It was in Byzantium that Andrew ordained Stachys as first Bishop of Byzantium (later Constantinople), thereby establishing an unbroken line of 276 Patriarchs down to the present day Patriarch Demitrios, who succeeded the renowned former Archbishop of North and South America, Athenagoras I. From Byzantium, Andrew went on to more glory through his compelling oratory and power of healing through Jesus Christ. He eventually found himself in Achaia, now known as Patras, on the west coast of Greece, where he was to suffer death as a martyr.

Andrew committed the grave crime in the eyes of the state of converting Maximilla, wife of the ruler Aegeates, to Christianity. Despite the fact that he was then eighty years old, it was ordered that he be put to death by being nailed upside down to an X-shaped cross. After three days of agony on this vile device, Andrew died. The great fisherman had cast his net for Christ for the last time.

The remains of St. Andrew were brought to Constantinople two hundred years later and in 1460 his head was given to the Pope by the defeated Mohammed II. It was in turn given to the people of Patras in an ecumenical gesture by the Pope on 24 September 1964.

December 1

St. Philaretos the Merciful

Membership in the exclusive society of saints is restricted to those Christians who have substantially aided the Christian endeavor. While it is true that the vast majority of our saints have been those whose service was a direct contribution to Christianity, one can find the company of the elite band of saints merely by acting as a Christian to an unusual degree in the course of a routine, secular life. A man whose only credentials for sainthood stemmed from his largesse holds out the hope for the average Christian, if not to become a saint, then at least to find favor with God through consideration of those less fortunate than others.

A man distinguished in his lifetime, save for the fact that he was born into a family of means, Philaretos was born in Amneia, about the middle of the eighth century, the son of a farmer whose land and stock holdings were extensive and whose Christian piety was genuine. Upon the untimely death of his father, he suddenly found himself sole owner of a sizeable estate, which he vowed to put to good use not for his personal gain, but for the good of the many impoverished whom he saw all about him and for whom he had a great deal of compassion.

The assets of the flourishing estate were directed to the needs of the poor and took form in the shape of philanthropic institutions for which Philaretos was principally responsible. His generosity became legendary in his own time and it was difficult to separate the wheat from the chaff in regards to the numbers who appealed to him for help and to whom he could never say no. In his eagerness to serve his fellow man he lost sight of the fact that he might one day fall victim to a turn in the tide of fortune, and indeed the day came when, owing to a number of adversities, he found himself stripped of everything he owned, with the exception of the house in which he lived. He managed to salvage his impressive home with the aid of friends and continued, outwardly at least, to live the lifestyle to which he and his family had been accustomed.

The magnificent house was mere facade, however, and Philaretos and his family experienced the deprivation of those he had assisted and his family bitterly complained that he had been generous to a fault. They complained that if this was to be his reward would have done better to look after his own welfare. The constant want gnawed at his once proud family and while they wavered in their faith, Philaretos remained unshaken in his and did his utmost to assure his family that God had not forsaken them. He tried to show them that in His own good time He would bring an end to their suffering.

It was in the midst of this prolonged misfortune that word came to the house of Philaretos that the Empress Irene herself was in the area and that she might favor the family with a visit to acknowledge the generosity of the master of the house about whom she had heard so much. When the Empress arrived, in the company of her son Constantine, the house was in readiness and great care had been taken not to expose the plight of the family whose pride had insisted that the decline of the family fortune remain a secret from the royal party.

The future Emperor Constantine looked with favor upon a niece of Philaretos who had come to help entertain the honored guests. Then and there, he decided to make her his bride, a decision which met with the approval of the Empress and which turned the tide of the affairs of the long suffering family. Invited to visit in turn at the Royal Palace in Constantinople, the generous Philaretos found that his reputation as a philanthropist had preceded him and he was enthusiastically greeted by persons in high places who eventually learned of his financial difficulties and saw to it that his estate was restored.

His faith in God thus vindicated, Philaretos and his family took up again the standard that had been snatched from them many years before. His benevolence continued to brighten the lives of the less fortunate and such was the extent of his kindness and true Christian spirit that after he died on 1 December 802, he was bestowed the honor of sainthood.

December 2

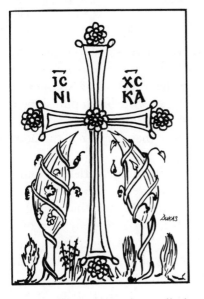

St. Myrope

The early centuries of Christianity witnessed so many
martyrs for Christ who may
have been overlooked by their
fellow Christians that it is
refreshing to discover an obscure saint who might in some
way epitomize all those who
have died for the Messiah
without recognition. Although
some martyrs may have died unnoticed by their fellow man, no
one has made the supreme sacrifice unnoticed by God. Such a
lesser light in the galaxy of those luminaries who have achieved
sainthood in the Christian Church was a wisp of a girl named
Myrope whose impact on Christianity may not have been in
the grand manner of a St. Helen, the mother of Constantine
the Great, but who nevertheless gave to the Lord her most
precious gift — her own life.

Myrope came from Ephesos, the city in which she was
baptized and in which the third century Christian community
flourished despite the shattering waves of persecutions that
periodically decimated their numbers. She grew to love the
Christian concept so greatly that she was drawn at an early
age to a convent near the tomb of St. Hermione, the martyred daughter of the Apostle Philip. The resting place of St.
Hermione would on occasion exude a miraculous holy myrrh
which the gentle Myrope would take to members of the faith,
hence her name Myrope.

During one of the more violent forays into the Christian
flock, Myrope fled with her mother to the comparative safety
of the Greek island of Chios, whose relative remoteness and
tranquility offered comfort to the beleaguered Christians. As
the mainland persecutions increased, the number of Christian
refugees on the island swelled to a proportion that was alarm-

ing to the state which had hitherto disregarded the peaceful island. The serenity was soon shattered by the presence of the imperial pagan ruler's soldiers under the direction of Noumerios, a man whose high rank was earned by swift, harsh punishment of Christians. Anxious to please the Emperor, he combed the hapless island in a reign of terror that paralyzed the community in fearful hiding.

During the siege an informer betrayed a young soldier to Noumerios, declaring him to be a secret believer in the Savior. This young soldier, Isidore, was summoned before the merciless Noumerios and told to disavow Christ or die by his own sword. Isidore chose to die and was thrown unceremoniously into a shallow grave. Guards were posted to insure that no Christian would remove the body for proper burial.

Myrope managed to slip past them in the dark of night and dragged the lifeless Isidore to waiting friends for the decent an honorable interment due him. Upon discovery of this the infuriated Noumerios ordered the guards to find the culprits or die in their place. The guards made a fruitless search and finally resigned themselves to death. When the news of this reached Myrope, she would not hear of anyone innocent, pagan or not, dying in her place and gave herself up to the authorities.

Noumerios marveled at the girl's complete honesty and courage and offered her a pardon if she would deny Christ and go on her way. When she refused, Noumerios sent her away with a shrug to whatever the prison officials chose to do. Visited daily in her dungeon cell by a jailer who repeated the offer, she rejected it again and again until she "offended the state" once too often. She was severely beaten and flung back into the cell, where she languished for many days before dying in agony of her wounds.

At the instant of her death holy myrrh began to flow from the dingy cell, filling the dungeon with a sweet aroma. Her jailer fell to his knees on the spot and accepted Christ. His more hardened cohorts quickly killed him also. Myrope gave her life for Christ on 12 December 250.

December 5

Saint Savvas

A certain way to avoid the glare of publicity, to never achieve a status that earns acclaim, in a word, to virtually assure complete obscurity, is to enter a monastery and shut yourself off from the outside world. While this is not the purpose for becoming a monk, nevertheless the conditions for notoriety remain the same and for a man to become famous while yet cloistered in a monastery is a tribute not only to the man, but to the noble purpose to which he is committed. Unnumbered thousands of God-fearing men have sequestered themselves in monasteries throughout the world, unheralded and unsung, but now and then one of their number stands out with special contribution to the Christian cause that gives him a renown he had not sought but richly deserves.

One such monk who eventually became a saint was a man names Savvas, who in his lifetime of service to Christ was accorded respect and tribute from not only his fellow monks but from the Christian community as well. He served with such distinction that he was given the title of St. Savvas the Consecrated in recognition of the deep respect with which he was regarded. Born in the 6th century, when Christianity was so frail its existence seemed doomed, Savvas became one of the monks to whom the Christian could look for spiritual uplifting and for support so vital to his cause. A remarkable scholar and profoundly religious figure, he had carved a reputation as a spiritual leader by the time he was 21 and stood out as one of Christianity's most prominent monastic personalities, conditioned to adversity and dedicated to the word of Christ in an eminent degree.

Having served with the highest honors at the monastery of Cappadocia for several years, he was summoned to the Holy

City of Jerusalem by St. Theoktistos to serve with another of the greatest monks of the day, St. Euthymios.This holy partnership proved itself virtually invincible in the crusade against intolerance, ignorance, and superstition. For Savvas it was to become a period of 65 years of unceasing effort in behalf of man and God during which time he founded many monasteries in Palestine and instituted the regimen for monasticism, which though severe by some standards, nevertheless was instrumental in producing the hardy breed of monks that were needed in the face of the open hostility toward Christianity. The structure of the Christian world would have been considerably eroded by the sinister forces about them had it not been for the dedication and courage of the monks of that day.

Savvas was called upon by many of the greatest religious minds to discourse on matters of dogma and it was he together with other leading figures of the time that staved off the heresies that lurked everywhere, seeking the Achilles heel of the Christian in vain. A master theologian, he was in the vanguard of those who protected the Church in the hour of its most severe trial, right up to the moment of his death at the age of 85, in about the year A.D. 540. He was laid to rest within the confines of the monastery of Jerusalem.

After the conquest of the Holy Land by the Moslem leader Saladin, it seemed hardly likely that anyone would recover the precious relics which the fleeing Christians had to leave behind, but in the Crusades that ensued the remains of St. Savvas were recovered and taken to the City of Venice and there enshrined in a cathedral, there to remain until 10 October 1965, at which time St. Savvas was returned at the direction of Pope Paul VI to the proper burial place at the monastery of Jerusalem. The ceremonial acceptance was made by Bishop Vasilios of Jerusalem who had gone to Venice at the direction of Patriarch Benedictos of Jerusalem.

Having served the Christian community for an ample lifetime, St. Savvas may, in being returned to the Holy City by the Church of Rome, be the instrument in death for bringing together the Eastern and Western branches of the Christian faith which have been apart since 1054 but who are now finding means, such as with the remains of St. Savvas, of bridging the long-standing gap that has separated them.

December 6

St. Nicholas

One of the most popular saints of the Christian Church of both the Greek East and the Latin West, St. Nicholas has in modern times been so inaccurately portrayed as a part of the Christmas scene that it is small wonder children do not confuse the celebration of the birth of Christ with that of the fat, white-bearded and jolly fellow so well publicized by enterprising merchants. Despite the fact that the feast day of St. Nicholas falls on December 6, he is not called to mind by any save the knowledgeable Orthodox until the 25th and the venerable saint, despite his association with the Savior, suffers as a result. The true greatness of this beloved saint is hidden in the shadows of legend, obscuring the identity of one of the most endearing of our saints.

Nothing is known of the early life of Nicholas, but it is known that he was born at the turn of the fourth century, during the reign of the Emperor Diocletian, in Asia Minor and was a bishop of Myra in that area which is now Turkey. Of a quiet and studious nature, he attended the Council of Nicaea in A.D. 325. On that momentous occasion he was so withdrawn that he is not even mentioned in the account of the proceedings recorded by St. Athanasios the Great; however, his behind the scenes activity did add to the luster of this memorable convocation. His importance was recognized by the Emperor Justinian, who had a magnificent cathedral erected in his memory in Constantinople.

Prior to his elevation as Archbishop, Nicholas had suffered imprisonment, harsh treatment and torture at the hands of the enemies of the Church. It was not until the reign of the Christian Emperor Constantine that he was able to lead the normal and peaceful life of a prelate. His leadership in Myra, which did not offer very hospitable surroundings for the Christians of the day, was so effective that his fame and popularity gave rise to many legends that were well intended but served only to screen the true character of this very real and industrious saint who labored for Christ all the years of his life, echoing the truth of Christianity uttered centuries before by the Apostles.

So great was St. Nicholas' popularity that he became the symbol of protection of children, which led to many of the legends about the man which have ultimately done more harm than good. After his death of natural causes at a venerable age, the legends and myths multiplied, but they only demonstrate how dearly loved he was for his great work. He became not only the patron saint of children, but also of merchants, sailors, and scholars, and was a protective symbol for travelers against highwaymen.

In a fascinating and daring enterprise in the late 11th century, the residents of Bari, Italy, where Nicholas' popularity had grown with the years, hatched a plot to recover the remains of the saint from Turkey. Through guile and ruse they were able to outwit the unwary but dangerous natives of Asia Minor and succeeded in removing the body of Saint Nicholas and transporting it back to Bari. There it was paraded in triumph through the streets before being properly enshrined on 9 May 1087, after which a magnificent basilica was erected in his honor.

In a rare ecumenical gesture, the Roman Catholic Church offered some relics of St. Nicholas to the Archdiocese of North and South America in 1972, where they repose in honored glory. Fragments of the saint's remains also repose on the altars of the Church of the Archangel in Stamford, Connecticut, the Archdiocesan Cathedral in New York, and the St. Nicholas Greek Orthodox Church in Flushing, New York.

The most widely accepted story of how St. Nicholas came to be associated with the gift-giving St. Nick is that which tells of how he secretly gave dowries to the three daughters of an impoverished parishoner, thus saving them from the disgrace that was the lot of the spinster of those days. Eventually, that carried over to the Christmas season and was associated with the Dutch Santa Claus. In fact he was generous to all people, but his fondness for children makes him especially revered.

December 7

St. Ambrose of Milan

The feast day of a saint is customarily observed on the day of his death, the day on which his spirit ascends into Heaven, but an exception to this rule is St. Ambrose of Milan, whose feast day is observed on the day he was consecrated a bishop because that event also was an unprecedented departure from customary procedure. Normally, years of service to Christ are required before a clergyman finally arrives to the office of bishop. However, St. Ambrose, a trained and effective lawyer who performed a great service to the Church through the power of his oratory, debarked from politics and entered the heart of the realm of religious service within an amazingly short period of time.

Born in Milan, Italy in A.D. 340, the son of the provincial governor of Gaul, Ambrose was heir to a legacy of government service, for which he was educated and trained in the family tradition. His advancement in politics was swift and his immense popularity led to his selection by the Emperor Valentinias as governor of Aemilia, Liguria. In this post he distinguished himself as an unbiased administrator, dedicated to the common good. An orator of consummate skill, he endeared himself to the community with his candor and high purpose.

When Bishop Auxentius of Milan, an iconoclastic Arian, died in A.D. 374, an anxious Christian community hoped for a successor free of the heretical teachings of Arianism. The ensuing conflict between the Orthodox and the Arians caused further dissent which threatened to lead to open hostility.

Ambrose was called upon to act as mediator, notwithstanding the fact that the unpleasant situation was religious and not political. In the course of bringing about harmony, Ambrose showed not only tact and diplomacy, but taking the Orthodox stand, he demonstrated deep religious conviction that had heretofore been dormant.

When it was suggested thereafter that Ambrose himself be made the bishop, the hierarchy did not take it too seriously, but when the clamor for Ambrose swelled into a loud mandate, the clergy could not ignore it and the mediator and champion of Orthodoxy was approached. Ambrose at first dismissed the idea, considering himself for one thing to be unworthy, but this only spurred the efforts to make him reconsider. After soul-searching meditation and extended discussion with members of the hierarchy, Ambrose accepted the proposal.

In a whirlwind of events, Ambrose was baptized at the age when his Savior was crucified, was ordained a deacon on 7 December 375, scarcely more than a year after the death of his predecessor, and was appointed Bishop of Milan. The importance of this date is stressed by the fact that December 7, a day that lives in infamy in United States history, lives in glory for Christianity and marks a triumph over heresy as well.

Bishop Ambrose was quick to acquire the knowledge required of a successful prelate and managed, along with his studies and administrative duties, to master the Greek language, which was a requirement for all who served as bishops no matter which corner of the empire they represented. The same popularity and influence that were his when he was a governor became his again in his service to Christ and over the years he wielded a great influence on the Christian community, all the way to the Emperor himself.

At one point Bishop Ambrose refused admittance to his Church to Emperor Theodosios and denied him the sacraments because the Emperor had authorized the slaughter of hostages seized in Salonica in retribution for the slaying of an officer in that city. A lesser prelate would not have dared such defiance, but Ambrose knew his position and in the end the Emperor repented and was readmitted to Christian worship. Bishop Ambrose died on 4 April 397.

December 16

St. Modestos

Since the birth of the Savior relatively few men of God who have found immortality in the sainthood of Christendom have emerged out of the Holy Land. It is almost as though the Holy Land, in yielding the Son of God, had been bereft of any further natural resources and had to content itself with lesser luminaries in the Christian Church. One of the exceptions to this seemingly barren ground of Christianity was a man named Modestos, who was born in Sebastia, Palestine during the reign of the Roman Emperor Maximinian (A.D. 292). His reign marked a time when the Christian population was sufficient to warrant a Patriarch of Jerusalem, an office which was to be ravaged in the coming centuries under the relentless assault by the Saracen hordes, among others.

The devout Christian parents of Modestos had about given up hope of ever having a child when their prayers to God for an offspring were finally answered with the birth of their only son, a son whom they were to know only briefly in infancy. At the height of an intensified persecution of Christians, the parents of the boy were taken from him when he was barely five months old and were put to death after a short imprisonment. It is said that the child was taken to the imperial household where he was placed in the custody of a childless couple in the royal retinue and raised in the pagan tradition.

When Modestos was 13 years old, however, he learned that he had been baptized a Christian and sought the company of a Christian goldsmith who taught the lad all he knew of Christianity and accepted him as his own, a gesture which made the two sons of the goldsmith envious. They plotted to rid themselves of the pious upstart. Several years older than Modestos, they contrived to have him sold into slavery. He was sent to serve a master in Egypt, where he remained for seven years, during which time he managed to convert the master and his entire household to Christianity. Given his freedom, he returned to Jerusalem.

Modestos had, since his introduction to the word of God, harbored a sincere desire to go to Mt. Sinai, where Moses had received the Ten Commandments from God. When at last this wish was fulfilled he made his way to a monastery, there to serve the Lord with an intensity of purpose that soon brought him to the attention of Church fathers and resulted in his ultimate ordination and assignment in the missionary work of Christ in all corners of the vast peninsula.

He had become the friend and confidant of Patriarch Platon of Jerusalem and when the ailing prelate saw that the end was near, he summoned Modestos to Jerusalem, along with members of the hierarchy. In accordance with tradition, a selection was to be made when some sign was given as to who should succeed the Patriarch. When the weakened prelate sought the comfort of the Church of Jerusalem, the huge iron gates were closed behind him. As each of the bishops approached, the gates failed to open for them. When Modestos put his hand to the latch the gate swung open. With this sign he was acclaimed the successor to the spiritual throne of Jerusalem.

Modestos, who lived to be 94 years old, served longer than any patriarch in history. During his time his spiritual leadership continued undiminished in the qualities of wisdom and piety that were manifested in the holy work to which he applied himself. Under his direction, many Christian shrines that had been destroyed by the Persian hordes were restored. Less known than other pillars of the Church, he nevertheless made a contribution to Christianity beyond measure and after his death was accorded the sainthood he so richly deserved.

December 21

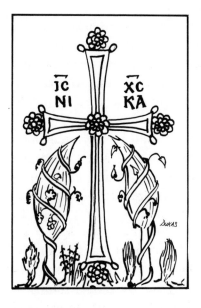

Juliane of Nikomedia

One of the saints who was to die in the fourth century for possessing Christian beliefs was a girl named Juliane, who was involved in no way with the activist Christian movement but who, nevertheless, achieved sainthood by a display of raw courage seldom evinced by one of her sex in stubbornly refusing to recant her beliefs. Utter courage is the trademark of the stoic male, but Juliane's stubborn valor in the face of insurmountable odds is an example of Christian fortitude not exceeded by the most stalwart male. Her contribution to the cause of Christianity in the fourth century, which witnessed some of Christendom's darkest hours, was equal to that of any of the untold numbers who died for Christ.

Born into wealth and station, Juliane was betrothed at an early age, as was the accepted custom of the day. She was scarcely nine years old when she was promised to become the wife of the prefect of the province who was more than willing to wait nine years for the girl who as a child was blessed with the rare combination of great intellect and extreme beauty. When she finally attained the age of eighteen she was a proficient scholar and a creature of delicate beauty. Despite her parents' paganism, she had accepted Christ as her Savior long before reaching a marriageable age and had been baptized by a monk who had introduced her to Christianity through the writings of St. Paul, the Apostle for whom she had the most abiding respect.

Deploring his paganism, Juliane nevertheless loved her

father and respected his wishes, not for one moment objecting to the pending marriage about which she had known for many years. She did not depart from the customary selection of a mate by the father, but she did object strenuously to becoming the bride of the prefect Eleusios, solely on the grounds that he was a pagan.

Eleusios was at first amused that his intended insisted on his becoming a Christian as a condition of marriage. Ultimatums were not given by prospective brides let alone to a prefect of the province. Not wishing to lose this prize, Eleusios joined the girl's father in an all-out effort to bring her back from the Christian fold, but no amount of pleading or cajolery could move her from her avowal as a follower of Jesus. Soon the enticement and frustrated pleading gave way to resentment and anger. The father, disgraced by his daughter's refusal to honor his commitment, turned her over to the prefect and walked away in disgust.

Eleusios, now master of the girl's fate, used every guile and cunning to get the lovely Juliane to renounce Christ. This she stubbornly refused to do no matter what was offered by the prefect. At last losing his composure completely, the wrathful Eleusios ordered the recalcitrant girl to be tossed into a dungeon, in which she was put to unspeakable indignities to break her spirit. The will which they sought to shatter showed not the slightest weakness. It became a cruel game of cat and mouse. She was put to torture of fiendish devices and when after all the prefect's tortures proved to no avail, her strong commitment to the Lord won over those who were trying by any means to wrest her from Jesus. It was evident that the Lord was with her when hot irons intended to brand her could not even produce a blemish.

Eleusios ordered the deaths of those who had openly confessed Christ and then had Juliane beheaded on 21 December 309. Her body was claimed by a pious widow whom none dared challenge and she was buried in a chapel on the outskirts of Nikomedia. It can be noted that Eleusios a short time later survived a shipwreck, but after making shore was consumed by wild beasts.

December 22nd

St. Anastasia (Pharmakolytria)

During the first four centuries of Christianity those
thousands faced persecution
with such indomitable courage
that they set the pattern for
centuries to come and assured
the steady growth of Christendom to the powerful force
which we take for granted
today. Difficult as it was to
remain a Christian during the dark hours of the pagan third
century, it was all but impossible for a woman to assert her
Christianity. Yet, these obstacles were overcome by a girl
named Anastasia who was cast in the classic Christian mold.

Anastasia was born in the eternal city of Rome, the daughter
of Pretextatos and Faust. She was of noble birth and belonged
to a family whose influence in the pagan Roman culture was
considerable. She was reared with every possible advantage.
Everything was chosen for Anastasia — everything but her
religion. Anastasia chose Christ, in spite of the influence of
her parents, who had not in the least considered the possibility
of their daughter's conversion to Christianity.

She became the wife of a man named Pouplios, who although
not of noble birth was nevertheless highly respected because of
his position as career diplomat in the Roman government. While
her husband attended to the affairs of state, Anastasia attended
to the needs of the suffering people of the Empire. A devout
Christian, she used the influence of her husband's position to
gain access to political and religious prisoners who languished
in the dungeons of Rome.

Her husband was killed by highwaymen en route to his new
assignment in Persia. After his death, Anastasia sold all of her
worldly possessions and distributed her wealth to the needy.

Since the observance of the Christian religion was in violation of Roman law, the jails and dungeons were overflowing with those who refused to deny Christ. More people died of starvation and disease than were actually put to death. Their poor bodies would have been thrown to the wolves and vultures were it not for the efforts of Anastasia, who worked tirelessly to see that these poor souls received Christian burials. She also cared for those who were still living with whatever medicines were available to the extent that she became known as Anastasia Pharmakolytria, the medicine woman.

When acts of piety, charity, and Christian service became a force to be reckoned with, the Roman Prefect had her summoned before him. He saw that she was no peasant swept off her feet by Christians, but a woman of noble birth, a traitor to her class, who knew her own mind and whose success would be Rome's downfall. Brushing aside the preliminary gestures, Anastasia was asked to renounce the Lord or face violent death. Anastasia, who had witnessed the agonies of countless prisoners, had firsthand knowledge of the atrocities of the dungeons, yet she never wavered in her choice of Christ.

After inhuman torment, she was put to death on 22 December 304. Later, her remains were buried in a chapel which was erected in her honor in Constantinople. For more than a millennium the chapel was her monument until the Turkish hordes destroyed it in the Ottoman invasion of 1453.

ALPHABETICAL INDEX OF SAINTS' NAMES